T0273117

# Freedom in Bondage

RANGJUNG YESHE BOOKS •
*www.rangjung.com*

PADMASAMBHAVA: *Treasures from Juniper Ridge* • *Advice from the Lotus-Born* • *Dakini Teachings* • *Following in Your Footsteps: The Lotus-Born Guru in Nepal* • *Following in Your Footsteps: The Lotus-Born Guru in India* • *Followig in Your Footsteps: The Lous-Born in Tibet, Vol. 3*

PADMASAMBHAVA AND JAMGÖN KONGTRÜL: *The Light of Wisdom, Vol. 1, Vol. 2, Vol. 3, Secret, Vol. 4 & Vol. 5*

PADMASAMBHAVA, CHOKGYUR LINGPA, JAMYANG KHYENTSE WANGPO, TULKU URGYEN RINPOCHE, ORGYEN TOBGYAL RINPOCHE, & OTHERS
*Dispeller of Obstacles* • *The Tara Compendium* • *Powerful Transformation* • *Dakini Activity*

YESHE TSOGYAL: *The Lotus-Born*

DAKPO TASHI NAMGYAL: *Clarifying the Natural State*

TSELE NATSOK RANGDRÖL: *Mirror of Mindfulness* • *Heart Lamp*

CHOKGYUR LINGPA: *Ocean of Amrita* • *The Great Gate* • *Skillful Grace* • *Great Accomplishment* • *Guru Heart Practices*

TRAKTUNG DUDJOM LINGPA: *A Clear Mirror*

JAMGÖN MIPHAM RINPOCHE: *Gateway to Knowledge, Vol. 1, Vol. 2, Vol. 3, & Vol. 4*

# Freedom in Bondage

## The Life and Teachings of
## Adeu Rinpoche

*Foreword by*
Tsoknyi Rinpoche

*Translated by*
Erik Pema Kunsang

*Compiled and edited by*
Marcia Binder Schmidt

Rangjung Yeshe Publications  2011

Rangjung Yeshe Publications
*www.rangjung.com*
*www.lotustreasure.com*

Rangjung Yeshe Publications
526 Entrada Dr. Apt. 201
Novato, CA 94949 USA

First edition 2011

1 3 5 7 9 8 6 4 2

Publication Data:

*Freedom In Bondage, The Life and Teachings of Adeu Rinpoche*
Translated from the Tibetan
by Erik Pema Kunsang (Erik Hein Schmidt).
Edited and compiled by Marcia Binder Schmidt

ISBN 978-962-7341-66-6 (pbk)
1. Religious Life—Buddhism 2. Buddhism—Doctrines
3. Vajrayana — Tibet. I. Title.

COVER. DESIGN: Maryann Lipaj

# Contents

# PREFACE

*Marcia Binder Schmidt*


The first time that I met Adeu Rinpoche was in 1989 up at Nagi Nunnery above the Kathmandu Valley in Nepal, when he had agreed to allow some of Tulku Urgyen Rinpoche's close, Western students to sit in on the empowerment of the *Three Sections of Dzogchen*, the *Dzogchen Desum*, a highly restricted, revealed treasure (*terma*) of Chokgyur Dechen Lingpa. This was no small acquiescence, since this empowerment is extremely profound and rare. Previously, the *Desum* had been passed down to only one or two people at any given transmission. The seal of secrecy had only been opened in Tulku Urgyen Rinpoche's generation.[1] The first time Chokgyur Lingpa bestowed the empowerment was to Jamyang Khyentse Wangpo and Tsewang Draka, the *tertön's* six-month-old son and reincarnation of Yudra Nyingpo, who in his past life was the foremost disciple of the great translator Vairotsana. The *Three Sections* was Vairotsana's heart essence and was entrusted to Yudra Nyingpo. That is also why Yudra Nyingpo's reincarnation, Tsewang Norbu, had to be the first to receive the empowerment.[2] Even the great master Jamgon Kongtrul did not receive the *Three Sections* the first time it was given.

My memories of Adeu Rinpoche from that time are rather vague, though I do remember that he seemed kind and gentle. Of course I had heard that he had spent many years in a Chinese prison camp, but aside from sitting in the same room with him for those five days, we did not interact much. It was not until nearly ten years later when I received teachings from him that his amazing lucidity and understanding became apparent to me. From then on, he became, after Tulku Urgyen Rinpoche, my most important and beloved teacher.

The selections gathered in this book, which span the period between 1999 and 2006, are but a small sampling of the profound and remarkable way in which Adeu Rinpoche imparted the Dharma. He gave instructions that were precise and rich in detail, yet simple and direct. His style reflected the depth of his experience, realization and compassion, as you will surely discover for yourself as you read his teachings. Adeu Rinpoche's own account of the time he was held in a Chinese prison camp was gathered primarily from conversations we had on a small island off the coast of China called Putoshan.

While at Putoshan, Rinpoche was asked how he was able to endure such terrible afflictions as unjust imprisonment and punishment without harboring any anger or resentment.

Over the next few days he recounted what he went through from the time of the Chinese crackdown in 1955, to his imprisonment and up until his release from prison in 1982.

During our three weeks together on the island, Adeu Rinpoche gave teachings four times a day: early morning in Tibetan, mid-morning and early afternoon with a translator for the Westerners, and in the evening he again taught the lamas.

Almost immediately these meetings aroused suspicion among the hotel staff. No one seemed to speak English, on the island, so, to get around, I asked for a guide. I was provided with a spunky young woman with nominal language skills who instantly decided that I was her new best friend and shadowed me for the rest of my stay. We later found out that she was the wife of the head of the secret police. Soon the hotel staff became increasingly uncomfortable and requested us to change rooms, but we refused. Finally they forced us out of our rooms for a couple of afternoons under the pretense that the rooms needed work.

During my various travels in remote areas of Tibet I have noticed that hotels typically only have a few rooms allocated for Westerners, even though there are many empty rooms that locals can rent. I suspect that the reason is that only certain rooms are wired with hidden microphones to record the occupants' conversations.

During the evenings, when the lamas were being taught, we Westerners would gather in one room and watch TV together. There was an incredible series on each night about Genghis Khan that, though spectacular in presentation, lacked any subtitles. So, each of us would take turns improvising what seemed to be appropriate dialogue for the action and dramatic visuals. Imagine my surprise several years later when one of the lamas who had been there told us that all this chatter had been dutifully taped and translated for the authorities. But we were pretty oblivious to this at the time, and continued with our teaching schedule, left the island, and returned to Shanghai where we prepared to depart to our respective destinations.

When we arrived at the airport, we came under tight surveillance and stringent searches of our luggage from very suspicious officials. In particular, the security officer who X-rayed my hand luggage glared at me relentlessly, spoke roughly and was convinced I was hiding something; I returned his aggression with similar disdain. As our eyes locked, I stared at him until he let the bag go with only one semi-careful search, which fortunately he did. As it turned out, I was the only one from our group to get out with any tapes; the others had theirs confiscated. We never did find out what we were suspected of. Nothing incriminating was found on the tapes, because none of us was in the slightest degree political.

As the years passed, given the possibility of retribution for those still living in Tibet, I doubted the idea of ever publishing any of this. However, after Rinpoche passed away in 2006, I reconsidered making this material available and concluded that Adeu Rinpoche told these stories in such detail with the idea of publishing them. What he says is not so much a criticism as a historical narrative and source of inspiration for others undergoing similar traumas. He never felt himself the victim and under all circumstances acted as a true practitioner, viewing all that happened as the play of karma and the opportunity to mingle Dharma with life exactly as it unfolded.

What distinguishes Adeu Rinpoche's story for me personally is not the horrors he endured under the Communist takeover of Tibet—he himself notes that many other people underwent much worse hardships, not to mention all those who died—but rather the way in which he told his tale. While describing what happened to him and to many others, how he had survived and finally obtained his release from prison, he spoke in a straightforward, dignified manner without any resentment, anger or sadness. He never added mental anguish to an already unbearable experience. Without blame or complaint, he viewed what happened to him as a ripening of his own individual karma, and thus courageously accepted responsibility for the abuse he suffered; in fact, he repeatedly stated that each person suffers according to his or her own karma. As Rinpoche mused, "I feel that whatever befalls you is a ripening of the specific karma that you created in the past."

Adeu Rinpoche took the trauma and suffering as an opportunity not only to accept the vicissitudes of life without bitterness, but also to transcend such unjust treatment by refusing to harbor ill-will against the perpetrators and instead developing compassion for them. In the end he turned suffering into happiness, for even while imprisoned he was able to meet many great masters, receive teachings from them, and even do some serious practice. It is truly inspiring that people exist in our world with such profound realization and accomplishment—they are examples to us all.

I only pray that releasing his tale together with some wonderful teachings will present a compassionate and wise face to the hardship Adeu Rinpoche and so many others endured and overcame with triumph. So, with humble gratitude to Adeu Rinpoche, I offer this banquet of realization, pith instruction and dignity with heartfelt love and appreciation, and the wish that it may be beneficial to all.

# Foreword

*Tsoknyi Rinpoche*

The first *Trulshik* Adeu Rinpoche was a student of the first Khamtrul Rinpoche. One day, while Khamtrul Rinpoche was at his retreat hermitage[3], even though he was in strict retreat and did not ordinarily receive any visitors, he told his attendants, "A man will come today, so whoever comes, just send him right up to meet me." That evening an exhausted man came and said, "I would like to see the lama." The attendants didn't think that Khamtrul Rinpoche could possibly have meant this guy, so they responded, "No, our lama is in retreat," and the man left.

Around dinnertime, when it was almost dark, Khamtrul Rinpoche asked his attendants if anybody had come. One said, "Well, a tired man came to see you but we told him you were in retreat." Rinpoche replied, "Oh, that's the man I need to see! Quick, go and find him!" It took the monk almost three hours before he caught up with Adeu Rinpoche and brought him back. Adeu Rinpoche went on to become Khamtrul Rinpoche's main student and an extremely great lama. The first part of Adeu Rinpoche's name, Trulshik, Destroyer of Delusion, comes from that time.

The author of this book is the eighth Adeu Rinpoche, and was born in Nangchen, Eastern Tibet. The Karmapa and Chögon Rinpoche together recognized him. Their letter of recognition is quite interesting, for they wrote that there's a place called "Ah", there's a family called "Ah", there are four or five "Ahs", exactly like (Ah) Adeu Rinpoche. By following these indications the incarnation was found. When Adeu Rinpoche was very young, many spiritual signs happened and then at three years old, he was sent to a monastery connected to the Nangchen Royal Palace where he trained and studied.

Adeu Rinpoche met and received teachings from many lamas, including Tulku Urgyen Rinpoche's uncle and root guru Samten Gyamtso as well as Chögon Rinpoche. Two of his main teachers were direct students of the great *togden* Shakya Shri.[4] His other teachers included special *khenpos* from Derge that Jamyang Khyentse Chökyi Lodro sent from his philosophical college at *Dzongsar*, one of whom was the main philosopher from the *Rimey* (non-sectarian) system.

As Samten Gyatso was the teacher to the King of Nangchen and the Royal family, he often came to *Nangchen Gar* where the palace and monastery were. Adeu Rinpoche received many Nyingma teachings and empowerments from him. Samten Gyamtso also gave Adeu Rinpoche his first pointing out instruction. Adeu Rinpoche really loved Samten Gyamtso. The day he heard that his root guru had passed away he thought, "My lama couldn't have passed away. He will show up again." For almost three weeks he couldn't believe it.

Adeu Rinpoche completed two full three-year retreats and knew practically everything! I've never met any other lama who knew so many different Buddhist topics. Whenever I had a question or someone else asked him something, he always knew the answer. Yet, he never put on airs of the highly learned or boasted about his knowledge. He knew smaller details like how to make perfect *tormas* and sand mandalas, and even how to carve. He also knew how to make medicine; however, he decided to give up medicine because it was too much for him to be both a doctor and lama at the same time.

He was also a poet and composed many beautiful texts. He was renowned for his writing, he would write a single draft and it would be perfect, free of any mistakes or errors.

He was also a tertön, a revealer of hidden treasures; and in this book he discusses the Guru Rinpoche practice he revealed. Sometimes his termas just came up in his mind and he could chant the whole text; for example, he didn't write his *guru sadhana*, it was a mind treasure. If he wrote a treasure down, he forgot it, so he had to memorize everything.

I met Adeu Rinpoche right after the Chokling Tersar empowerments Tulku Urgyen Rinpoche gave at Nagi Nunnery in 1986. I had a link with him from past lives, as the second Tsoknyi was one of Adeu Rinpoche's teachers. Adeu Rinpoche sent me many letters and Tulku Urgyen Rinpoche encouraged me to visit him in Tibet.

When I was twenty-one years old, I was a bit proud and arrogant. I went to Nangchen and stayed in the king's house. One morning people were busily moving about in the house and the King came with a long scarf and said, "Adeu Rinpoche may come to see you here. Offer him this scarf!" So while people rushed here and there, I dressed up nicely and waited.

I had already met Adeu Rinpoche but I had forgotten what he looked like. When I went to his room to meet him I thought that *this* couldn't be Adeu Rinpoche, because my mental image of him was of someone grandiose with a strong, powerful presence like Dilgo Khyentse Rinpoche, Khamtrul Rinpoche or the Karmapa, yet before me stood a small humble man. Everybody else was a bit scared of Adeu Rinpoche; they respected him immensely and were humbled by him. I, on the other hand, looked at him and thought, "He is not such a big deal." Also, his voice was not very loud; it was soft, sort of broken.

I offered him a white scarf, and he said, "Come in" and we sat down together. Then somehow as I looked at him, my perception shifted and I saw him as tall. Oddly enough, my pride slowly diminished and I felt myself becoming smaller and smaller, totally dissolving. His power was not in his physical body; it radiated from inside of him. Then I started to see that he was kind and open, yet dignified.

Over the years people had told me how great he was and that I should study with him but it didn't sink in. While Dilgo Khyentse Rinpoche and Tulku Urgyen Rinpoche were both alive, they preoccupied my mind. Eventually, I spent time with Adeu Rinpoche and all my arrogance disappeared, finally and I accepted him as my teacher.

I am glad I did. I learned many things and received numerous empowerments from him, including all the Ratna Lingpa empowerments, as well as those of the first Tsoknyi. My organization, Pundarika, sponsored and arranged for Adeu Rinpoche to bestow the *Six Yogas of Naropa* to representatives from thirty-five Drukpa Kagyü monasteries at an event I attended with eighty other yogis, khenpos, and tulkus.

Adeu Rinpoche and Khamtrul Rinpoche had received the entire Drukpa Kagyü lineage from Chögon Rinpoche at Nangchen Gar. They received these transmissions together over a period of nine months and then since Khamtrul Rinpoche died quite young, it fell to Adeu Rinpoche to pass them on. So when Adeu Rinpoche went to India, he stayed at Tashi Jong Monastery for a year and gave all the transmissions to the young Drukpa Kagyü tulkus, lamas, and monks.

Then Adeu Rinpoche went back to Kham where he spent another seven months passing on the entire set of Drukpa Kagyü teachings to all the tulkus, lamas, and monks there. After that he came back to Nepal to head the Drukpa Kagyü Heritage Project. He worked with me on inputting all the existing Drukpa Kagyü texts into the computer and correcting them in order to preserve, print, and distribute these to all the Drukpa Kagyü Monasteries. When in Nepal, Sengtrag Rinpoche asked him to give the complete Drukpa Kagyü cycle of empowerments, reading transmissions, and pith instructions, again, which he did at Ngedön Öseling Monastery.

Dilgo Khyentse Rinpoche had expressly ordered Adeu Rinpoche to take responsibility for the Drukpa Kagyü lineage, and Adeu Rinpoche transmitted everything at least three times; and now in Kham, Nepal, and India, the entire Drukpa Kagyü lineage passes through him. He was truly the main lineage holder of the Drukpa Kagyü of our time.

# Freedom in Bondage

## SHORT PRAYER BY ADEU RINPOCHE

Essence of the Buddhas in the three times, precious
   guru, hear me.
Grant your blessings to mature and liberate my
   being.
Grant your blessings that the special realization of
   the deepest path may dawn within my mind.
Grant your blessings that within this very life I may
   perfect the sublime path of the luminous Great
   Perfection.
Lord of every *siddha* family hear me,
Gaze upon me from the expanse of non-clinging
   and
   self-liberation.
As the treasure mind of uncontrived devotion
   overflows,
Let the world and beings be freed within the sphere
   of the three *kayas*.

# PART ONE: FREEDOM

I

# Devotion and Renunciation

Please form the resolve set upon attaining supreme enlightenment for the benefit of all sentient beings as numerous as the sky is vast, and continue to read while maintaining such an attitude.

From the start, every practice requires three steps: learning, reflection, and application. To begin with, we need to receive the teachings in an authentic way. Real learning involves gaining understanding about an instruction. To do this we need to hear it clearly from someone who is part of a living tradition, who has a true transmission for the teaching, and who can pass it on clearly. Having received the teaching, we then need to reflect upon it for ourselves. We need to gain some confidence and conviction about the value and methods of the teaching. Finally, we need to put the teaching to use by familiarizing ourselves with the practice and integrating it into our life. I want to stress this: after understanding a teaching intellectually and establishing it with certainty, it is vital to clear up any misconceptions and doubts you may have about it. Then you must make use of it in a very personal and intimate way, by practicing. This is where any teaching becomes effective—by actually practicing it, not simply knowing about it.

It does not work to simply know about a teaching and not use it. Mere intellectual knowledge is insufficient. It is the same as trying to cure a disease by simply reading about medicine, or by setting the medicine out on a table and looking at it, but not taking it. No one has ever been cured by merely looking at a bottle of medicine—you must take it. We must apply the treatment. Likewise, teachings are meant to be applied.

All the masters of both the Kagyü and Nyingma lineages have agreed that for a beginner on the spiritual path, compassion, devotion, and renunciation do not come naturally from one moment to the next. It simply does not happen like this at first. You must begin by forming the attitudes of compassion, devotion, and renunciation, and deliberately training in these. Over time, compassion, devotion, and renunciation will come more and more naturally, and no longer need to be contrived.

Renunciation, the will to be free, is a quality that every Dharma practitioner needs in order to progress on the path. Without it, you will not move forward. The first part of the general preliminaries helps to nurture this wish to be free. The four mind changings involve facing some unavoidable facts, so that you do not want anything other than freedom, and samsaric aims fall by the wayside very naturally. That is why the preliminaries are so vital to becoming a genuine Dharma practitioner. In Tibet it is said that a person who wants to be a Dharma practitioner but who has no sense of detachment from samsara, is like someone who builds a many-storied house on a frozen lake in the dead of winter. The structure may seem very solid, but when spring comes and the lake thaws, the whole building sinks. Similarly, you may appear to have a bit of steadiness in your practice, but without renunciation your practice crumbles as soon as difficulties or hardships arise. That is why Dharma practitioners should focus from the very beginning on detachment and renunciation, the will to be free.

In the past in Tibet, instruction manuals were designed in such a way that practitioners who started the preliminaries only received teachings on the first part. The teachings were then stopped until the students completed their practice. Teachings resumed when the students returned for the next instruction. After getting that instruction, students would go off and practice it, and so on, until they had completed both the general and specific preliminaries. Nothing was freely given in advance, and there was no assumption that you could practice at your own whim. If you didn't practice you didn't get instructions. The same method was used for the development stage of the *yidam* deity: you would receive instructions for a particular part of the practice, and then train in it. Having completed that, you would come back for more instructions. At the very least you needed to have completed the preliminaries before receiving instructions on *Dzogchen* or *Mahamudra*.

These days it appears to be a bit different. Many people want to skip everything and go directly to the completion stage. There are also those who, without having done any yidam practice or preliminaries, immediately want to do the yogic practices involving the subtle channels and energies. I, however, have great doubts about the effectiveness of such an approach—whether any actual understanding is developed, and whether this type of method is authentic and correct. Still, many people would like to jump ahead, skipping all the steps in between.

The Buddhist path is laid out in a progressive order from the very beginning. There is a particular reason for this. Having taken the first step, it is much easier to take the next because you are already a little ways along. Having completed the first step of the practice, you have already reached a certain level of accomplishment. It is then relatively simple to move on to the next level. That is why it was designed in this way. If people do not want to respect this system and try to skip ahead to unfamiliar places, difficulties will most likely occur.

You may receive a particular teaching, but you will need to apply it in practice—and I can guarantee that it will not be very easy to do so. It does not mean that it is impossible, but it requires a tremendous amount of perseverance. Many students do have a sincere interest in Dharma practice, yet in reality most people are not actually willing to apply the time and energy to do the necessary practices. It could be that after a while you find that nothing has happened, and you have not accomplished anything. At this point, it is quite easy to blame the teachings for not getting you anywhere, when in fact your impatience is to blame. Therefore, though you may find it occasionally frustrating, in reality it is probably more beneficial in the end to go step-by-step from the beginning.

Guru yoga is one of the most important of the preliminary practices. It is through guru yoga that we receive the blessings for the true transmission of realization. After reciting the supplications, receiving the four empowerments and mingling your mind with your teacher, you receive the blessings that enable you to connect with the view of the completion stage, which is not something that you can simply jump into without receiving an explanation.

There is a traditional saying from the great masters:

> Realization is reached through the path of
> blessings.
> Blessings are reached through the path of
> devotion.
> Devotion is reached through the path of
> supplication.

In other words, you cannot simply connect with the state of realization without any preparation. To realize original wakefulness, you need to connect with it through blessings, and blessings depend upon your own devotion, openness, and trust. You can cultivate these qualities through supplication, by bringing to mind the great qualities of your master, known as *the inexhaustible adornment wheel of the master's qualities*, and articulating your devotion in the form of a prayer or supplication. That is how devotion is brought forth, as well as how you receive the blessings and gain realization.

Jigten Sumgön, the great Drikung Kagyü master known as Lord of the Three Levels of Existence, wrote this verse:

> Unless the sunshine of your devotion
> Strikes the snow mountain of the guru's four
>     kayas
> The streams of blessing will not flow,
> So persevere in the practice of devotion.

Please recognize that if you want to realize the four *kayas* of the state of realization, you need to persevere in the openness of devotion; otherwise, it will not happen.

The Kagyü chant to Vajradhara, known as the *Dorje Chang Chungma*, says, "Devotion is the head of meditation, as is taught." Just as the most important part of the body is the head, without the head of devotion, there can be no meditation training.

The Indian siddha Saraha wrote a verse that said:

> Only by clearing the veils, creating merit,
> And receiving the blessings of a master most
>     sublime,

Will you realize the coemergent, the pristine and
    timeless wisdom;
Know therefore as delusion every other method's
    way.

It is simply folly to employ any other method to realize
the state of original wakefulness, such as trying to figure out
on your own what your basic nature is by using concepts. The
only path is that of blessings and devotion to a qualified master.
In the teachings of the Drugpa Kagyü lineage, there is
something called *the four sealed teachings*. The first one is the
view, which is Mahamudra; second is the meditation, which
is the Six Doctrines of Naropa; third is the conduct, which
is the six cycles of equal taste; and the fourth is the seven-
fold instruction on auspicious coincidence that is said to be
the ever-important guru yoga. Guru yoga is indispensable at
every single level of the path.

In the Drugpa Kagyü teachings, there is another saying, "It is questionable whether you can be liberated through
meditation, but there is no doubt that you can be liberated
through devotion." Of course, it is possible that simply studying and meditating might liberate someone, but the result is
not guaranteed. However, if you meditate with devotion to
your guru, then there is no doubt that you will be liberated.

Guru devotion and the practice of the guru sadhana
are strongly emphasized in the Nyingma teachings. Guru
Rinpoche also known as Padmasambhava said, "To realize
the guru is to realize the state of all the *sugatas*." This means

that if you realize his basic nature, then you realize the nature of all the buddhas, because the guru is the nature of all buddhas. This is why the guru sadhana is found among the termas of every major tertön.

The heart of the Buddhist path is training in original wakefulness, the state of equanimity, which is the basic meditation state itself. This is what we need to grow used to, and this is what the pointing-out instruction is all about. Simply put, your root guru is the one who bestows the pointing-out instruction, because no one else knows how to do it. The one who points out your nature in actuality is your vajra master. Thus, if you emphasize training in guru sadhana and guru devotion even before receiving the pointing-out instruction, it will have tremendous benefit.

Before we accept someone as our teacher and guide, all the scriptures, including the *Vajrayana tantras*, say that we need to examine whether that person is qualified to be a master. Blind acceptance of a teacher can be as harmful as unwittingly drinking poison. This is not only from the student's point of view. The lama must also examine whether the student is qualified as well, or else it could be quite harmful to both student and teacher. It is necessary for *both* teacher and student to be truly qualified.

In addition, the instruction must be effective. If these factors are complete, then the outcome will be authentic and perfect. It is important to clarify all of this before entering any kind of relationship with a Vajrayana teacher. First it is your own responsibility to check all of this carefully. It is not good enough to follow someone and find out once it is too late, because there are those who will lead you in the wrong direction if you just follow along blindly. This point is stated repeatedly in the teachings, and it is traditional to check beforehand. If not, we may find out that the teacher we have been following is not properly qualified, like discovering that the drink we imbibed was poisonous.

Likewise, the teacher needs to determine that the student is willing to apply the teachings thoroughly, and that he or she has the fortitude, courage, compassion, intelligence, and renunciation to carry on with perseverance. The individual might only be someone who is out "musk hunting," trying to get hold of a particular teaching in order to use it for selfish aims. Teachings are wasted on someone who never really applies them. Entering into such a relationship can be like jumping into an abyss: both teacher and student could end up in one of the hell realms.

Since all the scriptures state that we must be extremely careful in entering a teacher-student relationship maybe it is an important point! While you may not initially feel complete reverence and devotion to your teacher, you must try to develop it. In the beginning, devotion may be artificial but through the practice of opening up, you should get to the point where you appreciate that the guru's nature is identical to that of all the buddhas of the three times. Remember, in terms of kindness towards you, your guru's kindness is even greater than the Buddha's. Once you have developed that kind of devotion within your guru yoga practice, you are said to have established a firm foundation for the main practice of Mahamudra or Dzogchen.

# 2

# COHESIVE PRACTICE

The purpose of the very first session of the day
is to bring forth a strong sense of devotion and
renunciation. You focus on the guru, supplicate, and dissolve
the guru into yourself. What is the gauge of devotion? It when
tears come into your eyes and the hairs on your body stand up
and you sincerely feel real trust from the core of your innermost being. Likewise, with renunciation, go through the
contemplations one after the other, beginning with the reflection on the preciousness of this human body. Think about the
causes for having this opportunity to study and practice the
Buddhadharma, how rare this is and how few have it. Reflect
again and again until you become quite familiar with that
way of thinking and it becomes second nature to you. Only
when you really feel it and sincerely think, "I will not waste
any time; this really is an incredibly precious opportunity"

can you say that you have successfully fulfilled this contemplation.

Then without wasting any time whatsoever you should go on to the reflection on death and impermanence. Time is running out, so without becoming distracted and before moving on to the next one, karma cause and effect, you should contemplate each of the four mind changings until it takes effect and the real result is born in your mind[5].

Once you have genuinely gone through these four contemplations, you should be really scared of ending up in any of the lower realms. Picture yourself there, in one of the hell realms. "What would it feel like if I found myself there? What would it be like to suffer as a hungry ghost?" Imagine what it would be like to be an insect or an animal being eaten by others, starving for food, beaten, enslaved, or slaughtered. Really imagine yourself in such a predicament. You should actually feel the pain and suffering, so that you have an acute sense of "I want to be free. I don't want to end up in such a situation ever again." Only then should you go on to the next practice, which is taking refuge with true renunciation, meaning the will to be free.

Recite the refuge prayer from the core of your heart. Only when it has really taken effect, go on to the bodhisattva vow. First is aspiration and then application *bodhichitta*. Continue with this practice until it becomes a real sincere, deeply felt compassion, loving kindness and bodhichitta.

When I was young I went through these and some of my teachers made me spend ten days on each contemplation. Just as it is done in the separation of samsara and nirvana known as *khordey rushen*, I actually enacted each of the realms. I would imagine I was in one of the lower realms with such vividness that it seemed real, not just an idea. Once you have really integrated the contemplation into your being and have gone on to the next, then when you start a session, you only need to spend a short time on each of the previous ones.

After bodhichitta one enters the main part of the practice, which is called the *approach, close approach, accomplishment* and *great accomplishment,* i.e. visualization, recitation, and *samadhi.* The tradition is that one should practice each of these until certain signs occur, and only then do you proceed on to what comes after. In other words, each practice has a certain sign that is the measure of the training, such as sincerity, acute renunciation, devotion, compassion, and so forth. That is how it was practiced in the past, and how I practiced when I was young.

*Shamatha* practice is about taming this wild unruly mind, which, so to speak, needs to be restrained. When the mind is restrained; it stays put. However, with shamatha practice mind does not know itself, it is only confined so it doesn't fly off in one way or another. Training in shamatha means developing concentration, the fifth of the six *paramitas*, which has two aspects: with support and without support.

One such practice is to concentrate on a perfect support, such as the bodily form of the Buddha or Tara. To do this you place either a statue or a picture right in front of you, then you simply focus your attention on it in order to not be distracted. You now have a reference point so that it is easier to be aware of when your mind does wander off; and when it inevitably does, you simply refocus on the statue or image. The support does not necessarily have to be a material object; you can also close your eyes and visualize what Tara looks like and use that image as a support for not being distracted. Focusing on the pure image, whether actual or visualized, you can grow more and more familiar with being undistracted until you obtain the One-pointedness of shamatha.

In the beginning it is very beneficial to have a support, since the mind tends to be easily distracted. In our daily lives we don't even notice. However, be clear that, at this early stage, picturing Tara in one's mind is an act of thinking. Later on, this will be a conduit for recognizing mind essence, but at this point it is not *rigpa*. Shamatha lays the foundation for sustaining rigpa once your root guru has pointed out directly the nature of mind to you.

Student: How do we practice the six paramitas?

Rinpoche: To recognize the emptiness within any action —no matter how great or small—of the first five paramitas of generosity, patience, discipline, perseverance, and concentration is called embracing it with the sixth paramita, transcendental intelligence or wisdom. To do so entails having realized emptiness already and if that is the case then they are automatically embraced by emptiness and don't require any extra effort. However, if you are an ordinary person, then you can still embrace the five paramitas with the sixth by having a theoretical understanding of emptiness, which means viewing any action as an illusion.

It doesn't have to be perfect to begin with; most often one must mimic enlightened activity and understanding, and by so doing, accumulate the merit and wisdom necessary to achieve a true realization of emptiness. This is similar to doing sadhana practice when you picture something in your mind, chant the mantra while imagining that you send out rays of light, etc. This does not mean that you have mastered the development stage, but it is an excellent support. That is called devoted application. In the beginning you try your best and later, through dedication and perseverance, it becomes perfect.

STUDENT: How do we practice the two accumulations of merit and wisdom?

Rinpoche: The two accumulations of merit and wisdom should be practiced as a unity. Whenever you have done something good and worthwhile, then you just suspend all concepts about subject, object and action. By doing so, the accumulation of wisdom will then saturate the accumulation of merit and transform it into the accumulation of wisdom. That is how to transform one's actions. It is not like mixing two different things like water and milk, but rather sealing the relative with the ultimate.

Milarepa told Gampopa that when training in nonconceptual meditation, which is the accumulation of wisdom, if you then shift away to do conceptual practices like the accumulation of merit, there is a risk that the wisdom will slip away. Therefore, maintain nonconceptual meditation throughout all your activities whatever they might be.

Furthermore, Saraha said that just because one is training in the accumulation of wisdom doesn't mean that one should look down on the value of the accumulation of merit, because the accumulation of merit helps to strengthen and increase one's wisdom. Best is if there is always a balance between the two.

If you practice in a special place such as one of the sacred caves of Guru Rinpoche, you can increase any merit even more; or if you are with someone who is already creating vast merit, you can join in their activities and thus easily create a lot more merit. When provided with such opportunities, do not just turn your back thinking that it is all conceptual, because you can still embrace it with a nonconceptual view and transform it all into the accumulation of wisdom. However, if you are capable of remaining in non-conceptual composure you needn't give it up to create conceptual merit. Tilopa told his disciple Naropa, "My son, until you fully realize the indivisibility of emptiness and dependent origination, never remove either wheel from the chariot of merit and wisdom, but instead always practice them as a unity." There is a great purpose in always keeping the unity of merit and wisdom.

STUDENT: As practitioners of Mahamudra or Dzogchen, how should we behave?

Rinpoche: All schools of Tibetan Buddhism agree on the following four points: to attain certainty by means of the view, to practice by means of the meditation, to bring forth enhancement by means of the conduct, and to arrive at realization by means of the fruition.

Conduct is how a meditator should behave as his or her practice progresses. There are various types of conduct. In the beginning, it is essential to follow the Mahayana ideal of the bodhisattva, behaving in accordance with the six paramitas. Next comes "the ever-excellent conduct," then "the courageous awareness discipline," and finally "the completely victorious conduct." However the important thing is that we should act in accordance with our view so that our behavior and mode of conduct can assist and help deepen our realization of the view; otherwise it can be rather risky and dangerous.

If you lose your conduct in the view, then you could easily stray into deluded dissipation, by mistaking the continual stream of your own delusions for a high view. On the other hand, if your conduct is quite high but your view is not, then you will merely be acting like a realized yogi, rather than truly being one. Either way, turning your stream of being into a continuous flow of delusion is merely going to enmesh you further in samsara.

Guru Rinpoche said, "Do not lose the conduct in the view, rather be brave in the view and timid in your conduct." This means to recognize the highest view of Dzogchen, while still respecting the fine details of cause and effect by remaining fully aware that one's actions do have consequences.

Once when Paltrül Rinpoche was giving Dzogchen teachings to a group, one of his disciples would kill a sheep whenever he needed food. Paltrül Rinpoche called him in and said, "Hey! What are you doing? I hear you are killing sheep. Please explain yourself." "Well, sheep do not exist," his disciple replied, "and there is no one killing them either. The act of killing is a complete illusion and has no existence either." Hearing this Paltrül Rinpoche berated him for his arrogance and ignorance, for this guy was using the view as an excuse to justify his negative actions, demonstrating a complete misunderstanding of how to combine view and conduct. He had merely heard some Dzogchen teachings about the original nature of self-existing awareness itself not being subject to good and evil, not being affected by karma in any way whatsoever, and then he used this to make excuses for continuing his negative karmic actions. This is why it is said, "If one loses the conduct in the view it is possible to perpetuate the black demonic view of deluded dissipation." Please beware of this.

Another possible way to go astray is to hear the Dzogchen teachings, gain a bit of intellectual understanding, then think you've got it without doing anything further. It is not enough to just form an intellectual idea about the principles of Dzogchen without actually realizing the teachings in your personal experience or checking whether you actually are recognizing the view. That is nothing more than another way of deluding yourself.

There is a big difference between intellectual understanding, experience, and realization; we need to clearly distinguish how these three differ and why it is necessary to go through the progressive stages of the path. First to understand intellectually is to gain certainty and conviction by reflecting upon a practice. Thereafter apply it in one's experience to progress and arrive at realization. It is not enough to just form the assumption, "As I have heard the Dzogchen teachings, I am now a Dzogchen practitioner." Or even worse, "Since the Dzogchen practice is to not conceptualize, therefore I shouldn't meditate." Hearing the word "nonmeditation" some people mistakenly conclude that it is unnecessary to do anything whatsoever, and so deludedly believe that they do not have to practice at all.

Before he met Marpa, Milarepa met a Dzogchen master who told him, "I possess the instruction of the Great Perfection which, when you practice it in the morning you are a Buddha in the morning, if you practice it in the evening you are a Buddha in the evening. As a matter of fact if one has the continuity of former training one does not need to meditate at all but will still awaken to buddhahood." Hearing this Milarepa thought, "When practicing black magic it took me merely a week to attain signs of accomplishment. Later, conjuring up hailstorms took no more than a week either. So, obviously I am gifted. I must be a destined one. Therefore I don't need to meditate, since the master said a fortunate person doesn't need to practice and will still become enlightened. So I can just lean back and have a nap," and he lay down and snoozed. After a while the master called him back into his room to ask what had happened. Milarepa replied, "I have been taking it easy, resting and sleeping. As you said that I should consider myself a fortunate person, I figure there is no need for me to meditate." The Dzogchen master shook his head and said, "No, no, no! It seems you have no karmic connection with these teachings or me. You must go to see the translator Marpa, he is your karmically connected master." And he sent Milarepa off to study with Marpa. That's a good example of how one can misunderstand or miss the point altogether, so please be careful about your attitude and practice diligently.

# 3

## CORRELATING MAHAMUDRA AND DZOGCHEN<sup>6</sup>

The Mahamudra and Dzogchen systems are identical in essence—you may follow one or the other—yet each has unique instructions. Dzogchen has a particular set of teachings known as Tögal, and the approach of pointing out rigpa directly is found only in the Dzogchen teachings. Mahamudra is exceptional in the instructions known as the nine cycles of mingling. When embarking on meditation practice in the Mahamudra tradition, the meditator is taught three aspects: *stillness, occurrence,* and *noticing*.

The cultivation of stillness means to train in cutting off involvement in memories; you disengage from entertaining any thought about what has happened in the past. The same with regards to the future: you are not supposed to construct any plans about the next moment. And in the present, right now, simply and completely let go. Drop everything and settle into nowness. In the Mahamudra tradition, stillness refers to not following thoughts about the past, present or future—not churning out any new thoughts.

A beginner will notice that totally letting be without any thought involvement does not last that long. Due to the karmic force of the energy currents, new thoughts are continually formed—thoughts grasping at subject and object, at the pleasant and unpleasant. The activation of such patterns is known as occurrence.

When the attention is quiet and still, there is a knowing that this is so. When one is involved in thinking about this and that, there is a knowing that this is so. In this context of stillness and thought occurrence, this knowing is called noticing. These are the three aspects known as stillness, occurrence, and noticing.

Now, the training in Mahamudra is this: Each time you notice that you are thinking of something, you disengage from it and pull back—suspending your attention—into being quiet, into being still, and simply remain like that. When after a while you notice that you are thinking about something, again simply return to the stillness. That is the training. By repeating this over and over, you become more familiar, more experienced. That is how to progress.

As you grow more capable, there comes a point when the thought occurrences no longer have such a strong hold on the attention. It becomes easier to arrive back in quietness. Eventually, every time a thought begins to stir, rather than getting caught up in it, you will simply be able to remain, until the force of the thought occurrence weakens and the aware quality grows and strengthens. The dividing line between stillness and occurrence fades away. That is the point at which we can recognize the actual identity of noticing what mind nature really is. In other words, *vipashyana* can begin.

The great yogi Milarepa said, "In the gap between the past thought and the following thought, thought-free wakefulness continuously dawns." This is the way it is whether you recognize it or not, so the difference is to recognize. The opportunity to recognize is there all the time—the training is to do it.

In the beginning, a thought vanishes; that is called stillness. Next, a new thought arises; that is called thought occurrence. One notices that these are happening. These three—stillness, thought occurrence, and noticing—have to do with becoming increasingly aware of the gap between thoughts. This aware quality grows stronger and stronger, which only happens with training. You cannot artificially increase it. The difference between shamatha and vipashyana, in this context, is when you recognize that which notices and what the awake quality is.

According to the Dzogchen system, if your shamatha practice is simply training in being absentminded remaining in a neutral, indifferent state without any thought activity whatsoever, this is known as the all-ground. It is simply a way of being free of thought involvement. Moreover, when attention becomes active within the expanse of the all-ground that activity is known as dualistic mind. But when the dividing line between stillness and thought occurrence fades away, and instead the strength of the aware quality is intensified, the awake quality is known as rigpa. Depending on whether one is using the Mahamudra system or the Dzogchen approach, there are different terminologies, but the actual training is essentially the same in both cases.

According to the Dzogchen instructions, there are three points in regard to this context. First is tracking down dualistic mind, or the normal attention. Second is discovering the secret identity, dualistic mind's hidden way. Third is revealing its vanishing point. Tracking down means investigating how the attentive quality of dualistic mind behaves: where it comes from, where it is right now, and where it goes. The second point is actually finding out what it is, namely, a seeming presence—there is actually no *thing* there. It is just some behavior that is mistaken for being a real thing; actually there is no thing there whatsoever. It is only when we investigate that we discover that this attentive quality is not a thing, yet it has fooled us. It is called a nonexistent or seeming presence. The last point—revealing the vanishing point of dualistic mind—is that the moment you look into where this attentive quality is and what it is made of, you discover that there is no actual thing; it simply vanishes every time you look. This is the Dzogchen approach, to find out what dualistic mind really is.

This is how to discover and enter into the actuality of rigpa, because first we need to be clear about what dualistic mind is. Try to find out the identity of this awake quality that clings to reality. Where did mind come from? Where is it right now? When it is no more, where did it go? That is called inquiring into the arrival, remaining, and disappearance of dualistic mind.

This is the point when rigpa can be introduced or pointed out in actuality. The procedure, however, begins with shamatha, which is accompanied by certain experiences or meditative moods called *bliss*, *clarity*, and *nonthought*. Once one proceeds into the vipashyana quality in an uninterrupted way, so that one is no longer distractedly flitting here and there but has some ability to sustain that meditative state of mind, this is called *One-pointedness*, the first stage of Mahamudra. Continuing, you reach a level of progress known as *Simplicity*, which leads into another state known as *One Taste*, and finally you achieve a state known as *Nonmeditation*, or, literally, *non-cultivation*. This means that there is no longer anything that needs to be brought forth or cultivated by an agent cultivating it. In other words, the primordial state of enlightenment is discovered. Mind essence was pre-enlightened; our original ground is already enlightened. In the Dzogchen approach, this discovery is called being re-enlightened. Mahamudra does not use these terms re-enlightened and pre-enlightened, but at the fourth stage of Nonmeditation the meaning is basically the same.

The Dzogchen path begins with the actuality of rigpa being pointed out. This is like being shown the beginning of the road. One should not just stand there and wait, but must move forward. Sometimes people misunderstand and think that having received the pointing-out instruction and recognized rigpa in one's experience is enough and that they have achieved all there is to achieve. It is not sufficient however. Recognizing rigpa is only the beginning of the Dzogchen path. We need to follow through, and it requires a lot of perseverance. Giving the pointing-out instruction is like pointing to the ground and saying, "This is the road to Lhasa." If you just stand there, you will never get to Lhasa. You need to proceed step by step along the road, putting one foot in front of the other. Similarly, having recognized rigpa, you need to train and progress along the path. Of course you could say that the perseverance is effortless, but this definitely does not mean that we should ignore the need for practice. It is said that there are two types of Dzogchen practitioners: the lazy type and the diligent type. For the lazy type there is the practice of *Trekchö*, the training in primordial purity. For the diligent practitioner there is the *Tögal* path of training in spontaneous presence. But in both cases there is still the need to practice.

There are four stages of development in Dzogchen. The first stage comes with recognizing rigpa in actuality, which is sometimes called manifest dharmata or innate nature—the natural state seen as it actually is. As you progress and your experience deepens, it is called increased meditative experience. Third is awareness reaching fullness, and the fourth stage is called the exhaustion of all concepts and dualistic phenomena. This last stage is equivalent to the stage of Non-meditation in Mahamudra. As mentioned above, the ultimate state of enlightenment is being re-enlightened in the pre-enlightened original ground. The important Dzogchen master Paltrül Rinpoche often told his disciples, "You should leave room for progress. You should not think that you are already there and that there is nothing more to attain. Even though it is the state of rigpa, leave room for progress. Don't be satisfied yet; it is too early. There is still room for improvement in your practice."

What is pointed out according to the Mahamudra approach is the true state of original wakefulness as your ordinary mind. Once this has been pointed out to you, it is called mind-essence, and the instruction is: "Look into mind-essence. Sustain mind-essence. That is the way." According to the Dzogchen instructions, what is pointed out is called rigpa, which is the intrinsic original wakefulness that is present within you. You are then supposed to recognize rigpa and sustain it. There is no real difference between these two teachings. Of course, there are some extra instructions in the two systems. It is like approaching Bodhgaya from the south or the north: both roads lead to the same destination. The pointing-out instruction is the same as showing the unmistaken way that leads straight to Bodhgaya. If one truly recognizes the way one needs to train to be enlightened, then, if one follows this exactly, there is no doubt that this is the unmistaken path. However, one must still follow the path. How swiftly you reach the goal is entirely up to you and your diligence.

After having given Gampopa all the necessary instructions on meditation, Milarepa told him, "Now it is up to you to go and practice." As Gampopa was leaving, Milarepa accompanied him for a stretch. At one point he stopped and told Gampopa, "I have given you all the teachings, but there is one instruction I have held back." Gampopa thought he should make a mandala offering and made preparations to do so, to which Milarepa said, "There is no need to offer a mandala. I will just give you this teaching." Then he turned around, lifted his skirt, and bared his buttocks. They were so calloused that Gampopa could not tell whether they were made of flesh, stone, or wood. After he had given his student a good look, Milarepa said, "If you want to reach perfection in meditation practice, then you should sit as I have. I sat on solid stone continuously for so long that my butt is like a fossil—it's as hard as stone. You should train with this kind of perseverance. That is my last instruction." So it is not enough to just look at where you are standing and think that you have arrived somewhere else. The recognition of the awakened state of rigpa is not enlightenment but the path to enlightenment. You still need to develop the full strength of this recognition by continually training.

Now let's identify what we are actually supposed to train in during a meditation session. Generally this is said to be "natural" or "ordinary mind," but what is that? Does it mean our normal state of mind or the specific natural state of mind as described in the Great Perfection? The great tertön Sherab Özer said, "It is not enough to suspend your attention into not distinguishing between anything at all. Simply not meditating or keeping any concept of meditator or meditation object is not enough. This is likely just the vacant state of absentmindedness that is the basis for all of samsaric existence as well as nirvana."

According to Dzogchen one must identify the ground of liberation, the natural state of rigpa, which is not the same as the ordinary state of mind known as the all-ground. No matter how many thousands of years one trains in the state of the all-ground, there will be absolutely no progress—one will simply arise again in the state of samsara—whereas training in the natural state of mind of rigpa is nothing other than the ground of liberation. Therefore it is important to distinguish the normal, ordinary mind of the all-ground from the natural, ordinary mind that is the ground of liberation, and train accordingly. To put it simply, according to Dzogchen the self-knowing original wakefulness is pointed out in our ordinary state of mind.

According to Mahamudra, the essence of the meditation practice is found within the ordinary, natural state of mind; it is pointed out as the original, true wakefulness. Having recognized this, one can then proceed to train in it, and as the training deepens, there are certain stages of progress described as the four yogas, each of which is further divided into the three categories of lesser, medium and higher capacity. These are collectively known as the twelve aspects of the four yogas of the path of Mahamudra. Another approach is to apply the structure of the four yogas to each of the yogas, resulting in sixteen aspects. These are equally valid and merely describe the ever-deepening levels of experience and stability in the natural, ordinary mind.

The Dzogchen path has a similar explanation. According to Trekchö, there is a growing sense of becoming more and more accustomed to the state of rigpa, which is described as the stages of the path known as the four visions. These four can also be applied to the practice of Tögal.

But whether you follow Dzogchen or Mahamudra, please understand that ultimately there is no real difference. There is not one awakened state called Mahamudra and a separate one known as the Great Perfection. It is all of one taste within the expanse of *dharmakaya*. What these two words actually refer to is the basic nature of all things. Since all phenomena, all that appears and exists within samsara and nirvana, have the stamp of great bliss, it is called "the Great Seal," which is the literal meaning of Mahamudra. Similarly, since all phenomena are perfected in the expanse of self-existing awareness, it is called Dzogchen, or Great Perfection.

The fruition, the final result of the path, is described as awakening to true enlightenment within the expanse of the three kayas, in the sense that the empty essence is realized as dharmakaya, the cognizant nature is realized as *sambhogakaya*, and the ever-present capacity is realized as *nirmanakaya*. These three kayas are also realized to be indivisible within the single sphere of original wakefulness, and this holds true whether we call that state of fruition Mahamudra or Dzogchen.

# 4

# TRAINING

There are three statements:
Recognize the empty quality.
Train in the perceiving quality.
Practice their indivisibility.

Recognizing the empty quality means that you experience the empty identity of rigpa, which includes essence, nature, and capacity. In other words you recognize rigpa as it is. This is indispensable because you cannot train in what you have not recognized.

Training in the perceiving quality means that whatever objects appear to your field of perception, whatever takes place, sights and sounds and so forth, are experienced as thoughts going out towards objects. What we usually believe to be objects, in our field of experience, are just projections of an existence onto something that actually has no other subsistence than being a perception. Understanding the emptiness of object is simply letting go of ascribing a false existence to it. This is called sealing perceptions with emptiness or affixing the seal of emptiness onto perceptions.

Having recognized rigpa to be empty, then training with perceptions means recognizing that all perceptions are also empty. In other words, you recognize perceptions to be what they actually are and you no longer attach a fictitious reality to them as if they were real, concrete, external things. When training in emptiness, whatever unfolds from the nonexistent happens as an empty appearance free of grasping. In short, to "train in the perceiving quality" is to recognize the essence of mind within any appearances that arise.

The third statement, "practice their indivisibility," means to train in perception as a unity. At this stage you recognize that whatever you perceive has always been part of mind, so the dividing line between subject and object falls away. You are then naturally free of grasping and clinging. This corresponds to the level of Simplicity in Mahamudra.

When Milarepa received the pointing out instruction from Marpa, he showed that perceptions are mind, that mind is empty, and emptiness is dharmakaya—in other words, the mind and what it perceives are not separate at all: they are a unity. In Vajrayana the perceived represents the male aspect while the empty represents the female aspect. Also called means and knowledge, prajna and upaya, these are always seen as being an indivisible unity.

STUDENT: What are some of the stumbling blocks in the practice of rigpa?

Rinpoche: The most common stumbling blocks to maintaining the continuity of rigpa are the temporary experiences of bliss, clarity and nonthought. Let's take bliss as an example. This is when you are practicing and supposedly training in the natural state, but it has actually shifted into being a cozy state of shamatha where you feel extremely good. You get the feeling that, "I don't want to spill the soup because if I move, maybe I will ruin this state." It feels very comfortable, very smooth, very clear, and undisturbed. Being in such a state is so enjoyable that you don't even want to move a knee or arm, afraid that even the slightest movement will wreck that state. This is a sign that the mood of shamatha has saturated the state of rigpa and taken it over.

If this happens, you should totally disown that state. Instead of clinging to the meditation like a precious possession, you should toss it away, thinking "I don't need this." There is a statement that the mountain boulder improves by falling. It falls from a great height, clashes with stone, and gets polished and purified. Likewise, rushing water becomes fresher and purer as it flows downstream. In the same way the yogi's meditation is improved by destruction; repeatedly destroying the meditation state improves it.

The indication that one has slipped into shamatha is a sense of being attached or fascinated. Clinging, one goes astray. Rigpa is without clinging to anything whatsoever. It is wide open and clear, whereas shamatha doesn't have the lucidity to it. There is some lucidity but that is not like rigpa at all. Shamatha always has some attachment that is the difference. The further you go into the state of shamatha, the duller and sleepier you become. When that happens, just disrupt that meditation state and begin again; simply stop "meditating" and again start fresh.

In some of his songs Milarepa says that bliss, clarity, and nonthought are like the dregs of the view and should be thrown away. In other songs he says that bliss, clarity, and nonthought are like the summit of the view. How are these two seemingly contradictory statements reconciled? In the first case bliss, clarity, and nonthought are like the cozy mood or atmosphere of shamatha and so nothing more than a product of grasping mind. So of course such a state should to be dispensed with and not clung to. However the natural state, the essence itself is also blissful, clear, and free of thought, yet these qualities cannot be dispensed with because they are intrinsic to the natural state. The difference is that at the stage One-pointedness, one still clings to these temporary experiences; whereas in the next stage of Simplicity, they are recognized to be characteristics of the natural state which is not only blissful, clear, and free of thought, but also free of all clinging and grasping.

STUDENT: What exactly then is the difference between the bliss, clarity, and nonthought of shamatha with those of rigpa?

Rinpoche: Any experience arising from shamatha is but

a temporary meditation experience, while in the case of rigpa they are the flavors or attributes of knowing wakefulness itself, which is not a transitory phenomenon. The qualities of realization are unchanging, whereas the temporary experiences of shamatha do change. These temporary experiences may appear to obscure rigpa, but rigpa itself is actually free of all obscurations. Temporary experiences are like clouds in the sky, while rigpa is like the sky itself.

This unimpeded capacity is intrinsic to rigpa, like fire is hot and water is wet. There is no need to nail anything down, or prevent anything from happening; there is only one method and that is to maintain the continuity of rigpa. There is no other trick. As soon as the continuity of rigpa is lost, its capacity immediately strays into dualistic mind and a feeling of being disconnected from what is being perceived arises, and hence a seeming duality. As long as rigpa is left free its capacity remains ready. It is like the example of the mirror and the reflection; the mirror's capacity to reflect is not diminished by the reflection. It is a natural characteristic of a mirror to reflect.

However, when the capacity falls under the power of fixating, you stray into thought and lose sight of rigpa. Avoiding this is really quite simple: you merely do not stray from rigpa. Training involves nothing more than sustaining the continuity of rigpa. You do not need to create or do something; this capacity is already there automatically, because it is one of the three qualities of rigpa.

Do not do anything to prevent the unobstructed capacity of awareness from slipping away. It is always unimpeded and ready to perceive, it is an intrinsic quality of rigpa. Continuity lasts as long as rigpa doesn't stray from its own expanse. We can maintain the continuity of rigpa because rigpa is always within its own expanse. When straying from that continuity, then there is distraction or duality, so the only trick you need is to sustain the continuity. There is nothing other than that, no extra practice. To sustain the continuity just means to not lose rigpa's steadiness.

STUDENT: How does one clearly distinguish the awakened state of rigpa from a temporary experience of clarity?

Rinpoche: The difference is quite straightforward: As I mentioned repeatedly, temporary meditation experiences are transitory and hence change, they come and go, whereas rigpa doesn't fluctuate. However, to see this difference clearly you need to be certain that what you have been introduced to and recognized is rigpa to begin with. If you have recognized rigpa, clarified your doubts and gained certainty in your understanding then you should have no problem differentiating it from any temporary meditation experiences that arise.

Most temporary meditation experiences occur in the stages before you have gained stability in rigpa. When there is steadiness in rigpa, that steadiness doesn't get lost no matter what may unfold. You do not become caught up in any temporary experiences and they just naturally dissipate, like mist clearing. If on the other hand you are still unstable, then of course you will occasionally tend to get caught up in various experiences and moods.

So it is important not to cling, but to allow these experiences and moods to clear of their own accord, as in the famous saying, "Temporary meditation experiences are like mist; they fade and vanish, while realization is like the sky, unchanging."

STUDENT: Should one deliberately try to be fresher and invigorate one's senses?

Rinpoche: In some of the Drukpa Kagyü Mahamudra teachings, one should train in any situation, no matter whether one is clear or obscured. It shouldn't make any difference, so you should certainly try to invigorate yourself and be present. That is why it is always encouraged to practice in the pre-dawn when the sky is beginning to get light. To practice at that time is very important, especially by exhaling the stale breath many times.

To invigorate rigpa is called *hurjong* in Tibetan, which simply means letting rigpa be as it is. When you are about to get caught up in some temporary meditation mood you just focus on rigpa itself and rigpa then sustains its own strength. Rigpa is always itself and does not stray into anything else; this stability is called samadhi but really it's nothing other than the identity of rigpa itself, the awakened state. Rigpa can be described as the unshakeable knowing of itself. Knowing one's own empty identity, which is awake and self-aware, rigpa recognizes itself. Not straying from this would then be called the samadhi of rigpa. This is very different from the normal use of the word samadhi or shamatha. The normal usage of samadhi means a mental focus or concentration. This can be applied to many different contexts; for example, in any meditative state where something is being focused upon, the absence of straying from the object of attention is called samadhi.

Rigpa is very different from shamatha as it is defined by the lower vehicles. Rigpa is completely undefiled; it is untainted by even the subtlest of habitual tendencies. There is no clinging to anything at all; it is completely open and free. Therefore the normal sense of shamatha or samadhi doesn't apply to rigpa. However, in the context of rigpa, when clinging is not just absent but liberated, that is said to be the shamatha quality of rigpa. Samadhi is no other than rigpa naturally sustaining itself without wavering or distraction.

The awakened state of rigpa remains steady, it neither decreases nor increases; dullness and drowsiness only make it seem to diminish. An automatic dullness accompanies the tendency to want to rest in rigpa and safely settle there. When this happens you must reinvigorate yourself and liven yourself up.

The invigorating and disowning can be done together or separately it depends on the situation. Disowning is like taking a break. You part from the meditation state. For example, at the end of the session you don't hold on to it, you make dedication and then get up and go about your business. One of the great Drukpa Kagyü masters, Zangpo Gyari said, "At the end you always disown the meditation state." Invigorating is typically done as needed during the session. But if there is a need to free yourself from clinging to a particular state and then freshen up, then of course you can combine the two as appropriate.

# 5

# GURU YOGA

No matter which of the three vehicles you practice—Hinayana, Mahayana, or Mantrayana—from the moment you enter the gate of Buddha Shakyamuni's teachings until you attain complete enlightenment, you must have the support of a spiritual teacher in order to obtain the teachings. The *pratimoksha* precepts of individual liberation need to be given by a preceptor who possesses the twelve qualities of spiritual training according to the shravaka level. The bodhisattva vow is transmitted by a holder of that vow, someone whose stream-of-being is saturated by bodhichitta and thus worthy of giving the vow to others. Vajrayana teachings must be received from a vajra master who has earned the title by demonstrating a degree of accomplishment in the stages of development and completion. Only a master with the blessings of the lineage can transmit the Vajrayana teachings. No matter what level of practice you pursue, you cannot really progress by groping in the dark or trying to figure it out by yourself. Merely trying to use your own intellect to decipher the path to enlightenment lacks the true blessings of the lineage.

Right now, as we are unable to meet the Buddha in person, we must learn from someone who represents the Buddha and teaches what the Buddha taught. From our perspective, in terms of kindness, such a person is superior to Buddha Shakyamuni, for, unlike the Buddha, this is the person we meet and from whom we can receive teachings. Hence, you must first acknowledge your personal guru's kindness as the communicator of the Buddha's teachings.

If you have already set out on the Buddhist path by taking refuge and are determined to proceed onward to attain complete enlightenment, it does not help to walk blindly, seeking direction by chance, nor does it make sense to follow someone who does not know the path. You need a guide who has traveled the same path and can tell you how to proceed. If you are sincere about attaining enlightenment, then whichever level you want to practice—whether pratimoksha, bodhisattva, or Mantra—it is indispensable to find a capable spiritual guide.

First, be skilled in examining the teacher; second, be skilled in following the teacher; and third, be skilled in absorbing his or her state of realization or wisdom mind. Learn how to evaluate the person from whom you are about to take guidance. Once you feel confidence in this person, study how to follow him or her. Lastly, assimilate or train in your teacher's state of realization.

Before following anyone, you need to first examine that person to determine whether he or she is actually competent and possesses the prescribed qualifications according to the pratimoksha, bodhisattva, or tantric level. But once you have decided to follow a particular teacher, it does not help to continue to judge him or her, trying to figure out whether you made the right choice. Such an attitude will only pollute your mind. Instead, after making a positive assessment and choosing to follow a teacher, simply do so. Remember, it is your responsibility to check carefully whether a potential teacher is qualified, holds a lineage, and has received blessings. Only after becoming confident that this is so, and feeling that you can really trust this person and can keep pure *samaya* or sacred commitment with him or her, should you ask for the appropriate teachings.

What if you later find out that you were mistaken, that the teacher is not trustworthy, and that he or she is not guiding you toward liberation but is pointing you in the wrong direction? Someone who guides people in the opposite direction of liberation is, by definition, not a spiritual teacher but a corrupter and unqualified, and there is no duty to follow blindly merely because you accepted him or her to begin with. It is perfectly alright to find somebody else. Especially today, all kinds of people present themselves as spiritual teachers. If you run into one of these charlatans, you should avoid them. On the other hand, if you do have a true teacher but somehow develop a negative attitude and destroy your connection with that person, this is the same as rejecting the Dharma, and it will have severe repercussions.

Not only should you examine the teacher, you should also scrutinize yourself. Even if you have a precious human body possessing the eight freedoms and ten riches, you still need to be truthful about your level of sincerity. Examine yourself honestly. You need to determine whether you are willing to follow a teacher sincerely and do whatever he or she recommends, rather than merely acting as if you are going to do so. Learn all about the shravaka precepts, the bodhisattva trainings, the tantric commitments, and what they entail. Then ask yourself, "Am I really willing to abide by them?" Check your level of resolve and determination and your level of fortitude and perseverance. Are you prepared to go through with this? Once you connect with a teacher, you should follow his or her instructions. If you are directed to do something, are you really willing to do it? You need to determine this beforehand, to avoid merely pretending that you are going to follow the prescribed path.

The teachings about the necessity of a teacher are well known in all the Buddhist scriptures; for example, there is the statement that one thousand buddhas of this aeon all have spiritual teachers of their own. The word *buddha* would not even appear in the world if there were no spiritual teachers. In other words, a teacher is indispensable.

The connection between you and your spiritual guide is of utmost seriousness. Your relationship with that person makes or breaks your spiritual development. In fact, as you progress through the vehicles, the relationship between you and your teacher becomes increasingly crucial. For example, the bodhisattva's connection to a teacher is more profound than the shravaka's, and if you want to follow the path of Vajrayana, the relationship is even more vital. In Vajrayana, it is by means of a master that you proceed to enlightenment. Your ultimate root guru introduces you to your innate state of wisdom, pointing it out to you. This is the most significant person you could possibly meet. Attaining buddhahood is due to training in this ultimate wakefulness; and the only way you can wind up in the hell of incessant torment is by destroying the connection with your teacher. So you could say that the highest risk as well as the greatest benefit depends on the person of the utmost importance—your ultimate root guru. That makes him or her a very significant person.

Once you feel confident in your choice, the next step is knowing how to follow the spiritual guide. That is something you can and should learn very carefully. How to behave in your relationship with the spiritual master is defined precisely in the sutras and tantras. How to honor, respect, and act around your teacher, as well as how to treat your guru and how to request teachings are all explained therein. You should check whether you are actually adhering to all of these suggestions, and then adjust your behavior accordingly.

As I mentioned, when relating to a guru, you should be skilled in three things: first, examining the guru; second, following the guru; and third, absorbing his or her state of realization, the wisdom mind. I have covered the first point. What about the second point?

Following a guru can be done in different ways: The best way is by practice and realization; the next-best is by serving your guru with your body and voice; and the third-best is by offering material things. Each of these ways of honoring your master directly relates to and brings you closer to a particular level of practice.

Milarepa is regarded as Tibet's greatest yogi. He was able, in a single lifetime, to overcome the depths of samsara and attain complete realization. He is the highest example of someone who honored his own master by one-pointedly practicing what he was taught. He is also the foremost example of serving a master with body and speech. He obeyed every command Marpa uttered, without any hesitation or mistrust. No matter how much Marpa abused or scolded him, putting him through severe trials, Milarepa never lost faith for even one instant. When he was refused teaching, instead of turning against Marpa, he blamed himself for not having enough merit. Even though he came to the brink of despair, he never once turned against Marpa. Hence Milarepa is considered the highest example of how to follow one's teacher wholeheartedly.

Another way of serving the guru is by making material offerings. Tsang-Yang Gyatso, a disciple of the first Tsoknyi Rinpoche, exemplifies this. He began as a layperson and later became a monk at my monastery. At the age of forty, he met Tsoknyi Rinpoche. Several times during his life he offered his teacher every single possession he owned, not keeping even a teacup or an extra set of clothes. When he accumulated more possessions, he gave everything away again. After the third time of giving all he had, his guru said, "That's enough. You have completed the accumulation of merit now. I can guarantee you that." He is an example of someone who was able to honor the guru with material things.

Kyobpa Jigten Sumgön, one of the early Drikung Kagyü masters, had tens of thousands of disciples. One day, a group of them wanted to present their realization as an offering to their guru. Not only did they explain their level of realization, they each performed a miracle in front of him to demonstrate their level of practice. Meanwhile, the master's cook thought, "I worked hard here in the kitchen and never had time to do even a single practice session. All I have ever produced is food and tea, so I have nothing to show." He sat there, miserable and depressed. The master knew his thoughts and said, "Hey, cook, stand up! I am sure you have something to show." And sure enough, when the cook stood up, he not only left a footprint in the stone floor, he also levitated. The others complained, "Hey, wait a minute! We did all this practice while this guy only cooked. How can he perform miracles like that without any practice?" Their master replied, "Don't think that serving with body and voice is not practice. Real practice means to surrender and follow the guru's wishes in whatever way one can. So even cooking can be practice. That is probably why the blessings of realization have entered his stream-of-being."

Finally, you must become skilled in assimilating the guru's state of realization, his or her wisdom mind, which is the source of all the qualities the guru embodies. In addition to practicing and serving the guru, following the guru means imitating him or her in all ways: emulating the guru's behavior—how he or she treats others, even how he or she dresses and walks—and trying to adopt the flavor or quality of the guru's being. Now, to assimilate the guru's realization means first to understand exactly who your guru is. Find out how he or she trained, received teachings, practiced those teachings, and developed his or her practice; what kind of experience and realization the guru has, what his or her accomplishments are, and what qualities he or she has manifested, as well as his or her virtues and absence of flaws. You need to know something about all of these.

Once you find out who your guru actually is, then compare yourself in every single aspect. When you have discovered how your guru trained and what he or she learned and realized, ask yourself, "What am I actually doing and what have I really done? What have I learned, what have I practiced, what have I understood and realized?" Examine yourself minutely in comparison with your guru. If you don't do this, you might think, "Well, he is a human being, and I am a human being. He eats and sleeps and dresses, and so do I. We both have needs; we are pretty much alike. Maybe he is a little better, but we are basically the same." In the long run it is not enough merely to feel admiration, which will never turn into profound devotion; devotion is necessary because it allows you to receive blessings. In fact, there can be no blessings without devotion.

Unfortunately, devotion does not come spontaneously. It is not a given that you will automatically have the requisite pure appreciation of your teacher. He may simply be someone you are fond of; therefore, you may need to work at engendering devotion. Just as it is mandatory to discover what the mind is in order to be able to remain in the natural state, you must know how to give rise to a genuine feeling of devotion in order to receive blessings. There are many teachings that explain how to generate devotion when it is lacking, such as the *Profound Path*, a famous manual of the Drukpa Kagyü School.

To perceive the guru as a buddha in person, it is necessary to reflect upon the guru's superior qualities. In other words, truly understand that he or she is extraordinary. The guru is not at all like you. If you are honest about it, free of all pretense and duplicity, you will become aware of what your stream-of-being usually is: one harmful emotion after another. This bundle of *skandhas,* aggregates, is a continuous stream of negativity. The guru, on the other hand, is someone who realizes the path to complete enlightenment. This difference is immense. If you sincerely understand this difference, then real devotion may arise, and you will begin to yearn to assimilate similar qualities. It is essential to motivate yourself with a strong wish and determination to follow in the guru's footsteps and attain the same level. This is a point of exceptional importance.

So, if devotion is lacking, it needs to be created. Later, when you truly see the qualities of the lama, unfabricated devotion will arise of its own accord. To attain the level of your guru, first you need devotion. If devotion is not there in the beginning, develop it. Once you have trained in devotion and feel it, then it doesn't matter what kind of guru yoga practice you do. It can be an extensive or condensed version, but in either case if you lack devotion, the blessings of the Dharma will never enter your stream-of-being.

It is said that if you see the guru as just a person, then

when receiving nectar from the vase, you will perceive only water, nothing else. If you perceive your guru as an ordinary human being, you will attain only the state of an ordinary human being. However, if you can perceive your guru as a buddha, you can become a buddha. If you perceive your guru as a siddha, you can become a siddha. The level you will be able to achieve is whatever level you perceive your guru to be.

When I was in a Chinese prison camp, I met a *geshe* named Gyamtso. He was a follower of a teacher from Drepung named Drayu Dorje Chang, who was the single most important Gelugpa lineage master of his time. Everyone from Sera, Drepung, and Ganden monasteries had received empowerments and teachings from him. Gyamtso had learned a lot from this teacher. He told me the following story. Drayu Dorje Chang was giving teachings to a large gathering of important incarnate lamas, geshes, and senior monks at Drepung, one of the greatest Gelugpa monasteries in central Tibet.

"Today," he began, "I have something important to ask you, and I want you to be honest with me. Will you give me a sincere reply?" He joined his palms, and they wondered what he was going to ask. He then continued, "In this snowy land of Tibet, the four traditions of Buddhist teachings— Gelugpa, Kagyü, Sakya and Nyingma—are all equal, and all follow the same teacher, Buddha Shakyamuni. There is no difference there; that is for certain. Each of these four schools possesses the complete path of Sutra and Tantra and the methods on how to attain complete enlightenment. They are all equal—there is no difference there, either. But the last time someone in our lineage attained the celestial realm, (going to the buddhafield in a physical body) was a very long time ago." The teacher mentioned an early Kadampa master. "Since then I haven't heard of that happening in the Gelugpa lineage. It seems like a very rare occurrence. But in the Kagyü and Nyingma schools, even these days there are numerous stories of people either attaining the rainbow body or going straight to the buddha realms in a physical body. So tell me frankly, if we have the same teachings and we are following the same teacher, why do some traditions have more, you could say, *visible* attainments and others have fewer? What is the difference?"

He joined his palms and looked at everybody, waiting for an answer, but nobody said a word.

After a while, Drayu Dorje Chang spoke again. "Well, if you are not going to say anything, maybe I can propose an answer, and then you can at least tell me if I am correct."

There was a moment of silence. He then quoted two lines from a tantra called the *Togpa Dünpa:*[7] "The simple-minded person with faith will be closer to enlightenment, while the intellectual who scrutinizes will have no accomplishment." He then said, "As I understand this, no matter how you go about it, trust or faith is the one decisive factor for all these occurrences of accomplishments that you see in the Kagyü and Nyingma lineages. It is because they emphasize guru yoga as the most vital practice, the indispensable entrance door to realization. By supplicating, generating devotion and receiving blessings, they attain realization. In my humble opinion, that is why the Kagyü and Nyingma lineages have so many practitioners who have attained accomplishments. What do you think?" Again, nobody uttered a word.

Gyamtso told me this story to illustrate the extraordinary qualities of guru yoga.

In the writings of the early Drukpa Kagyü masters such as Götsangpa, Lorepa, Yangönpa, Barawa, and many others, you find the statement that single-minded devotion is of utmost importance. They put a lot of emphasis on how to first generate devotion and then, after having given rise to devotion, how to stabilize it. Finally, there are teachings on how to attain realization by means of steady devotion and practicing guru yoga.

To begin training in guru yoga, first you need to check yourself to see whether you have any devotion. Next you need to learn how to give rise to devotion in your heart and to cultivate it. Then gradually, as you train more and more, you will receive the compassionate power of blessings in actuality. In all the teachings of Vajrayana, you will find that guru yoga is considered to be the most important practice. Developing devotion through guru yoga is sufficient unto itself, but without it no path will be successful.

As I said, even though we have connected with a spiritual master, if we take an honest look at ourselves, we must admit that we are merely ordinary people. We need refinement, and the way to improve and nurture ourselves is to go through certain trainings by which we can develop the will to be free of samsaric existence. According to our own disposition, we aim either toward the higher realms within samsara, the definite goodness of liberation, or toward complete enlightenment.

The way to develop true renunciation is described in most of the scriptures, including the *Light of Wisdom* and the *Essential Instruction on the Threefold Excellence.*[8] Start by reflecting on the four mind changings, which comprise the general preliminaries. Subsequently, train in the specific preliminaries, taking refuge, forming the bodhisattva resolve, and so on. Different chants are used in different traditions, yet the intent and meaning are the same whether the preliminaries belong to the old or the new schools. Use the text that you were given by your own teacher. The key point is to practice and persevere in making yourself a suitable recipient for the teachings. All the Buddhist lineages teach a form of guru yoga practice. Sometimes it is considered a preliminary, sometimes the main part, but either way it remains the entrance door for the blessings, the empowerments, and so forth. Guru yoga is the universal practice.

The main part of practice is simply an extension of the preliminaries. This is equally true for the general preliminaries of the four mind changings and the special, extraordinary preliminaries called *ngöndro*. The preliminaries are the common foundation for all schools; whether Nyingma or Sarma, there is no difference. It is the insight you gain during the preliminaries that becomes the main part of practice, and it is within the preliminaries that guru yoga is found in a short, simple form.

Guru yoga opens the door of blessings. There can be no

realization without blessings, no blessings without devotion, and no devotion without supplication. However, supplication does not simply mean chanting, but opening up from the core of your heart. When there is devotion in your innermost heart, you receive the blessings, and receiving the blessings makes realization possible. This is the purpose of guru yoga, very concisely put.

The Nyingma and Sarma schools have many guru yoga practices of varying lengths. Look at it this way: when you taste molasses, whether it is a large amount or small, it still tastes sweet. Likewise, however long or short the practice is, the key point remains the same: to receive the blessings.

It should also be noted that in yidam practice, the guru is in the form of a particular deity. It is said that by realizing one sugata, all buddhas are realized. In other words, if you accomplish one guru, you accomplish all buddhas. It is like what Padmasambhava says in the terma teachings of *Barchey Künsel*, "If you realize me, you realize all buddhas. If you behold me, you behold all buddhas." In other words, you see all buddhas in actuality. You can realize all enlightened ones, all yidams and so forth, by realizing a single one.

Naturally, realization of the guru is also realization of the yidam, as illustrated in this story from Marpa's biography. Naropa once manifested the mandala of Hevajra so clearly that Marpa could see the central figure appear on the shrine. He then asked Marpa, "Well, now, from whom do you prefer to receive the blessings, the substance of the accomplishment—me or the yidam?" Marpa thought, "I'm with the guru all the time, but seeing the yidam in actuality is a unique opportunity." So, he bowed to the shrine. Naropa then reabsorbed the Hevajra deity back into his heart center and said, "Now to whom are you going to prostrate?" This story shows that every yidam deity is the manifestation of the guru. And remember that you do not receive more blessings from an extensive practice and fewer blessings from a short practice. In both cases, the blessings are exactly the same—it all depends on your sincerity and the strength of your devotion.

Tilopa once told Naropa that everything is included within guru sadhana, even removing hindrances and bringing forth enhancement. Tilopa said, "While supplicating, combine the object, thought, and substance into one." The object here refers to the sublime object, the root guru. The thought is the willingness to accomplish whatever your guru commands down to the letter. This willingness to persevere is the brave attitude to continue with the practice no matter what. Finally, the substance is the state of realization and behavior that the guru embodies, which should be assimilated into your own stream-of-being. Ultimately, it is by realizing the guru's mind, the play of original wakefulness, that you truly mingle the guru's mind with your own.

The general advice is to study as much and as broadly as possible. But when combining everything into your own practice, condense it into these three principles. First, be skilled in examining the teacher; next, be skilled in following the teacher; and third, be skilled in assimilating the teacher's realization. All the different levels of Buddhism recommend including everything in a single practice. Here is a story to illustrate this point.

My incarnation lineage is also called Trülshik. The third Trülshik used to chant the supplication to the guru for almost any purpose. The prayer begins, "All sentient beings, my mothers infinite in number, supplicate the nirmanakaya guru," and continues with one line for each of the four kayas. If this lama were called to somebody's house to do *phowa* near the dead body, he would go there, put his hand on the corpse's head, and recite these four lines. After he had chanted them three or four times, there would invariably be some visible sign. For example, people would see a rainbow radiating from the body, or a bit of the hair would fall out.

He would do the same chant for other purposes as well. One autumn, he went with his disciples to collect alms, but they ran into bandits who took everything from them, including their pack animals. How did the guru react? He chanted the same supplication to the guru, "All sentient beings, my mothers infinite in number, supplicate the nirmanakaya guru . . ." The disciples were a bit upset, and behind his back they grumbled, "He *never* chants anything else. Maybe he doesn't know any other prayer." Anyway, the next morning, much to everyone's surprise, the bandits came and gave everything back. It seems that while the bandits were cooking parts of one of the animals, they looked in the pot and all of a sudden saw nothing but clear water. There was suddenly no meat. Other strange things occurred as well, and they got very scared and thought, "Wait a minute! Maybe we robbed the wrong lama!" So they went and returned everything they had taken, saying, "Keep this— we don't want any of it!" Then the disciples said among themselves, "Our lama may know only one chant, but at least it works!"

In fact this lama had attained complete mastery, and it did not really matter what he chanted. Based on guru yoga, from within his wisdom mind, his state of realization, he could carry out all activities. He did not have to do specific practices for different purposes.

This is also what Gyalwa Yangönpa, an earlier Drukpa Kagyü master, said: "Among all the different practices that I have taught you, there is only one that suffices for all purposes. I can guarantee that one practice: guru yoga." Everything can be included within this single practice—all aspects of both development stage and completion stage, as well as the inner yogas of channels, energies, and essences.

There are various ways to practice guru yoga. There is the way of accomplishing the guru according to the nirmanakaya level, according to the sambhogakaya level, according to the dharmakaya level, and finally according to the level of the essence body, the svabhavikakaya. For example, in the traditions of both Ratna Lingpa's termas and the *Profound Path* of the Drukpa Kagyü, when one practices all four levels of guru yoga, it is at the sambhogakaya level that the subtle yogic practices are included. Additionally, in our Drukpa Kagyü tradition, there is a set of teachings called *The Five Command Seals*. These are the view of Mahamudra, the meditation of Naropa's Six Doctrines, the conduct of equal taste, the fruition that manifests as auspicious coincidence, and then the ever-vital guru yoga.

The practice of guru yoga is essentially the same in all

traditions. One begins with the outer methods of realizing the guru through guru sadhana, namely, paying respect by bowing down over and over, by making offerings such as mandala offerings, and the various other ways of gathering the accumulations. Next there is the inner practice of guru yoga with the Three Roots as the guru principle. Here the guru embodies the essence of the Three Jewels and Three Roots, the lama, the yidam deity and the protector or dakini. After this comes the innermost way, in which the main point is to regard the yidam as being in essence the guru. Then the yidam and recitation of mantra are used to realize the guru's mind.

Whether the sadhana is long or short, it always includes receiving the blessings in the form of the four empowerments. Empowerment, from the Sanskrit *abhisheka*, means "dispersing and anointing," in the sense of purifying the veils of obscurations and becoming imbued with the enlightened qualities. That is what it all comes down to. What you recite for this, too, can be either brief or extensive, but what you visualize is always the same: You imagine that the four levels of obscurations are cleared away and you receive the four empowerments authorizing you to practice the four levels of the path and implanting the seeds for the ultimate fruition of the four kayas within your stream-of-being.

Please understand that no matter what you chant or visualize, the vital point of guru yoga is to train in receiving the four empowerments repeatedly at the end of the session. This is the entrance door to the blessings for the extraordinary and special teachings. After the empowerments, in some form or other, every text says, "Now settle evenly in the state in which the guru's mind and your own are indivisible as one taste." What does "settle evenly" mean? If you are a beginner who doesn't know what the guru's mind is, then do as the master Karma Chagmey instructs: "Just imagine that whatever the guru's mind is, is also now yours. No more and no less, as if you are stamped from the same mold. Your state of mind is identical with the guru's." Merely feel confident that this is so, and remain without interruption by any thought about this or that, past, present, or future. After remaining like that for a while, dedicate the merit. According to Karma Chagmey, that is good enough for a beginner. Just feel confident that the guru's mind and your own are now one.

If you have already been introduced to the state of rigpa, then you can have a different type of confidence. On one side there is the guru's mind, which is identical with that of dharmakaya Samantabhadra, and on the other, there is your own buddha nature that is present as the ground nature of your mind. These two do not differ in the slightest, neither in size nor in quality. Like space mingling with space, your mind mingles with that of your guru, so as to be indivisible, of one taste. Be confident that your realized mind and your guru's are no different. Then settle into the state of equanimity.

At this point there are two options: you can imagine either that your entire being dissolves into the guru, or that you have now obtained every single enlightened quality that the guru possesses, without a single exception. Whether you imagine your normal state of mind dissolving into the ultimate wisdom, or that ultimate wisdom is transferred into your own stream-of-being, which is the final transmission, so that you are able to realize the state of the guru's mind as indivisible from your own, either of these ways of settling into equanimity is fine.

To reiterate, first you receive the four empowerments and then you mingle your mind with the guru's and settle in equanimity—completely and utterly letting go. Practice whichever method you know best, it is an individual matter; but whatever you do, feel confident that you have received all the blessings, and then let be.

As you progress on the path, your devotion should become as steady as your stability in self-existing awareness. According to Paltrül Rinpoche, "To gauge your level of realization, you could of course go and present it as an offering to a master, but that is not always necessary. Instead you can be your own judge and offer your realization to yourself.[9] Authenticate it in this simple way: as you go along training in the composure of awareness, if you notice that you have more trust and devotion, more compassion, less attachment, and more renunciation, kindness and so forth, then I can assure you that you are moving along the correct path. However, if you notice that you are becoming more insensitive, that you do not trust any master you meet, that the more time you spend with your guru the less appreciation you have for him, you don't care whether sentient beings suffer or not, and you are more unfeeling and cold, then I can certify that you are moving in the wrong direction. Meditating while continuing along the wrong track will bring no benefit whatsoever, as it is not a direct cause for enlightenment. This is how you can see for yourself whether your practice is going well. In short, devotion and compassion increase as stability in rigpa improves.

Finally, what is really meant by "root guru"? Whomever you receive teachings from is the root guru for that particular teaching. For example, if you received the details of development and completion stage of a yidam from a specific teacher, then he or she is your root guru for that particular yidam practice. The ultimate root guru, however, is the one who gives the pointing-out instruction so that you recognize the nature of mind. That person is the true root guru because he or she has taught you how to attain complete realization.

Whether you practice guru sadhana on the outer, inner, or innermost level, or in the ultimate manner of simplicity, you should keep the goal—the expanse of naked awareness—clearly in mind. In other words, whether you call your practice Mahamudra or Dzogchen, and whichever level you are at, you are still aiming at the same goal. The guru's mind, having realized rigpa in actuality, is the state of mind you are to mingle with. The guru is the vehicle for arriving at the realization that the guru's mind and your own are in nature indivisible. This is the ultimate guru yoga taught in all the different traditions.

Tulku Urgyen Rinpoche's *Ultimate Guru Sadhana of Simplicity* belongs to that type of guru yoga. It is the way to realize the dharmakaya level of mingling the guru's mind and your own. In that sense it is identical with the *Tigle Gyachen,*[10] which is the innermost unexcelled level of practice in the Nyingtig tradition. There are many other similar practices as well, and they are all equal in identifying that the awakened state that the guru has realized and your own state of rigpa are not different in any way whatsoever. Training in the state of rigpa is the ultimate guru yoga, the real guru yoga.

# 6

# MINDFULNESS

The Mahamudra system refers to four types of
mindfulness, the first of which is deliberate
mindfulness. This coincides with the first of the four yogas of
Mahamudra, One-pointedness. Here we try hard to be mindful and make a deliberate effort to be present. After growing accustomed to the sense of being mindful, the mindful
presence evolves so that it requires less effort and there is no
difference between the occurrence of thoughts and stillness,
and we progress to the next level. That is the time of Simplicity, which is the second of the four yogas. When practicing
Simplicity, mindfulness becomes effortless. As our practice progresses, the object, which is the nature of mind, and
being present are no longer perceived to be two different
entities. The third type of mindfulness is called true or perfect mindfulness and corresponds to the third stage of One

Taste. Finally, the identities of that which is being cultivated and that which cultivates are not different whatsoever. At this stage, mindfulness is nothing more than a label and it is known as the king of supreme mindfulness. This occurs at the time of Nonmeditation, the last of the four yogas of Mahamudra.

There is a quote in the Dzogchen tradition that states, "While undistracted, when you release without meditating, even being mindful is still the innate state." This means that when letting totally be without being distracted and without trying to cultivate anything, simply releasing everything, without speculating, without discriminating, without thinking, without imagining either, the mindful presence is then not something other than the innate nature, the dharmata itself.

The peerless master Gampopa wrote four very precious lines that summarize all this:

> This primordially pure mind is the creator of
>     both samsara and nirvana,
> Leave it without fabrication in the state of
>     composure.
> Non-distraction is the path of all the Buddhas.
> There is nothing else to cultivate, so resolve on
>     watchfulness itself.

The first two lines refer to the meditation session. The last two refer to the time between formal sessions, which is commonly referred to as the post-meditation state.

The Tibetan word for mindfulness is *drenpa*, but here Gampopa uses the term *drentsi,* which means watchfulness, like a shepherd keeping an eye on his flock without really controlling their movements. There is nothing to cultivate other than that, so simply resolve on being watchful.

During your meditation sessions take support of watchfulness and in the breaks between sessions do the same. Basically, all throughout the day, whether sitting on your meditation cushion or going about your daily activities you should continuously train in sustaining *watchfulness.* As you grow more and more familiar by practicing during formal sessions, it will come easier during the rest of your day. Sometimes remembering your guru or some other situation can trigger it, and then suddenly you recognize the natural state. When this happens, nothing more needs to be done: you simply let it be. It is not like a formal session that has a beginning, middle and end; or like a sadhana where you follow a text. You simply let it be, naturally resting in that state.

Attaining stability in the recognition of rigpa comes about by being more present, through *drentsi,* maintaining mindful presence. The spontaneous recognition of rigpa is the best kind; the more you train in being present, the more often it will arise of its own accord, until the state of rigpa becomes continuous, seamless, and unbroken throughout day and night. As it is said, "There is no division between sessions and breaks, no separation between composure and post-meditation."

This is the result of applying mindfulness in your own life. If you want to be more mindful, you must try to be more mindful. There is no trick other than applying yourself to being more mindful in all situations.

Here is a simple way of clarifying what is meant by mindfulness (*drenpa*). In the beginning, you attempt to be mindful, to be present by making an effort to hold your mind. There is a strong sense of clinging and being really aware—this is deliberate or effortful mindfulness. By practicing in this way, over time the grasping within mindful presence slowly loosens and the necessary effort diminishes in kind. If one perseveres then eventually mindfulness becomes effortless and sustains itself, which in the Mahamudra tradition corresponds to the level of Simplicity, the absence of constructs.

At this stage it still feels as if there is a state being maintained and a subject maintaining it, but actually these are not two separate things but a unity. Eventually even that appearance falls away and merges into one taste, which is the true mindfulness. This, then, is the state of Nonmeditation: when cultivating, being mindful, and mindfulness itself are all totally transcended.

At the beginning, however, it seems that unless you deliberately try to keep mindfulness then the meditation state slips away. For most people a kind of subtle daydreaming, known as the undercurrent of thought, seeps in; you are just sitting there concentrating and, without even noticing, the next thing you know you are thinking about this and that and your meditation has slipped away. Therefore, there is a need to be deliberately mindful and present; but as time goes on, that need becomes less and less.

There is a statement that, "In the all-pervasiveness of

open space there is neither something to remember nor anything to forget." It totally transcends any notion of meditating, cultivating or being mindful. As Dungso Repa said, "I trained and trained in the innate nature just as my guru asked me to, but now I am at a loss as to what to train in. Both the training and that to be cultivated have disappeared." In other words, his meditation had gone missing.

> QUESTION: Sometimes it appears that there is an observer, a watcher, so how does one dissolve this sense of separateness?

Rinpoche: It only seems that there is an observer being watchful, but in reality there is not. There is a no actual duality, it just seems like there is. What we call watchfulness or attentiveness here is simply not forgetting, not being distracted. It is only a resemblance of duality.

> QUESTION: Eventually does even the resemblance vanish?

Rinpoche: In the practice of training in sustaining the continuity of mind essence, that which recognizes the continuity of mind essence, and the mind essence being maintained, are not different entities. This is not a mere theory; the experience of it is exactly like that. At the beginning you are instructed to notice whether there is thought occurrence or whether the mind is quiet. In both of these situations it feels as if the noticing is separate from the thoughts or the stillness;

yet actually that isn't the case. It only seems as if the mind that notices is separate from the thinking and from the stillness. But if you look into the identity of these, you will discover that they are not separate at all. Similarly, it only seems as if there is a subject and object when sustaining mind essence, but in reality these are not two different entities. Recognizing this in actuality is called sustaining the continuity.

In the beginning, when being aware of this continuity, it may appear as though there is someone watching and something being observed, as if there is a continuity being sustained and an act of sustaining it. However, that is not how it is at all, because these two have the same identity. According to Paltrül Rinpoche, rigpa is both the observer and the observed.

# 7

# MINGLING

Typically, while going about our daily activities between meditation sessions we become distracted, and our awareness is lost. If there is no recognition of rigpa, then one is no different from anyone else. When rising from a session of training in rigpa during the meditation state, the ensuing wakefulness (*yeshe*) can linger. When this happens, even though you interact with other people, the state of equanimity and an ongoing wakefulness remain. During ensuing wakefulness there is no coarse or blatant involvement in deluded states of mind, any thought that occurs is immediately, spontaneously liberated. This is a state of mind permeated with the flavor of knowing mind essence; you cannot say that it is the meditation state, nor can you say that it is not the meditation state.

No matter what practice you do, you always conclude

your sessions; nonetheless, it is important to carry away a sense of mindful presence. The ensuing wakefulness should be brought into your daily activities. If there is mindful presence, the ensuing wakefulness can continue. The moment mindful presence is lost, the ensuing wakefulness vanishes too. No matter what level of teaching you practice, it is very important always to bring this unobstructed quality into your daily activities. You mingle the practice with daily activities simply by never parting from mindful presence. Be present, rather than absentminded.

Whether you are practicing development stage or completion stage, presence of mind is always necessary and should be maintained continuously. In the case of the development stage, after dissolving the mandala and the deity, you reappear again [as the deity], then go about your daily tasks. Maintain the simple confident pride of being the deity throughout all your activities. Never part from this mindful presence, engage in life but be present at the same time. This is not like the more common types of shamatha where you are occupied by the practice and state of shamatha itself. Here the most important thing is not to be preoccupied, but sustain an unobstructed state of mind while being mindfully present.

When training in rigpa, in original wakefulness completely free of duality, there is still some mindful or present quality—the ensuing wakefulness—that continues between sessions. Due to this atmosphere of ensuing wakefulness, it is absolutely certain that training in rigpa will make you clearer; so even after you have closed your session by dedicating merit, etc., do not depart from this state of mind that is lucid, unobstructed, and not preoccupied by anything.

How successful you are at this depends on how much you have practiced—how familiar you have become with the natural state. There has to be a mindful presence, but to determine if it really is the expression of rigpa depends on how familiar you are with the state of rigpa and how much stability you have gained. If you are very stable then whatever you do takes place within rigpa, but until then it is good to alternate between formal sessions and daily life activities. Masters of both the Mahamudra and Dzogchen traditions recommend short moments repeated many times, in other words you spend a little while in equanimity, then do some daily activities and then stop and meditate for a bit more and then go back to your tasks.

The expression of awareness takes the form of the intelligence that fully discerns phenomena. Without parting from rigpa, everything is known clearly and distinctly. This quality is actually there from the very beginning. It is part of the ground, for the basic nature itself has the ability to discern everything and is always present; however, it is not necessarily manifest. Through training, it manifests more and more, but in essence, it is fundamentally, already present—that is why it is called original wakefulness, or basic wakefulness.

The intelligence that fully discerns all phenomena is the essence of awareness, like the light of a flame or heat of a fire. Therefore it is not actually a question of attaining this intelligence, because it is already primordially present in every state, whether samsara or nirvana. This is the quality of the ground: it is fully present; there is no state that is not saturated by it. Now, however it is obscured by dualistic mind, so one must train in order to fully realize its presence in actuality.

As a beginner, you lack stability in awareness, but are on the path, interested and even devoted to rigpa. However, once rigpa has become stabilized, then awareness dissolves into the great wisdom expanse and is like the sun and its rays—it will pervade all of samsara and nirvana.

Let's be clear however: right now, while on the path, you are under the influence of dualistic mind. Whatever you are engaged in—writing, for example—is the working of dualistic mind. Yet when rigpa has been stabilized, then all activities will unfold as an expression of awareness. Then even writing can unfold as Paltrül Rinpoche describes in his colophon to *Three Words That Strike the Vital Point*. He says that these lines were brought out of the treasure mind of the dharmakaya by the treasure revealer of the expression of rigpa. This may sound like a distant dream for you, yet if you train diligently it is definitely possible. The strength of your training determines whether ordinary intelligence is transcended or not.

*Togden* means to be realized, knowing everything; you are wiser. Being truly realized means that the moments of involvement in deluded thinking dissolve more and more often. Deluded thinking lessens and discursive thought is dissolved in the state of rigpa. That is a sign of having evolved in practice.

In order to further my own progress while I was in the concentration camp, I received an instruction called *mingling the threefold sky* from a realized yogi, Lama Rigzin. You do this practice from time to time in order to overcome hindrances in the training of *Trekchö*; for example, when you feel obscured due to drowsiness or dullness you do it to lift the veil, so to speak. It is not necessarily a continuous practice, but something you apply when required.

Lama Rigzin explained it as follows. "When mingling the threefold space, the outer sky is the space outside, the inner sky is the interruption of the flow of thinking, the empty essence and innermost sky is the unimpededness of rigpa, awareness. Mingling actually just means allowing these to be of indivisible one taste. The mingling, and where it is mingled, is in rigpa. When recognizing rigpa, these three "skies" automatically intermingle, for they are actually already one within the expanse of rigpa; however, allowing these three to be of indivisible one taste is nevertheless called mingling the threefold sky.

While we were in prison, Khenpo Munsel told me an interesting story about how his teacher Nyoshul Lungtog requested a teaching from Paltrül Rinpoche on how to mingle the threefold sky. It was early evening and the sun had already set. Paltrül Rinpoche got up and said, "Come with me." They went outside, where Paltrül Rinpoche sat down in a meadow and told Nyoshul Lungtog to join him. Nyushul Lungtog did what he was told and sat down. Paltrül Rinpoche said, "Fall flat on your back." Paltrül Rinpoche fell backwards and so did Nyoshul Lungtog. "Just spread out your arms and legs, like a spread eagle," Paltrül Rinpoche said. Nyoshul Lungtog did so.

"Do you see that there are no clouds in the sky?" Paltrül Rinpoche asked. "It is completely wide open," Nyoshul Lungtog agreed. After a while Paltrül Rinpoche said, "Do you hear the dogs barking at the monastery?"

"Yeah," affirmed Nyoshul Lungtog.

"Do you hear the sound of the spring water in the distance?"

"Yeah."

"Okay, just let all of that be, without it being separated in any way whatsoever, completely in one taste," Paltrül Rinpoche explained. "That's it. Just leave it all wide open."

> Student: Is the practice of equalizing as one taste different or the same as recognizing the natural state?

Rinpoche: There is a difference in level. The equalizing of one taste, such as equalizing pleasure and pain, is on a more general level, whereas rigpa is a different stage that has to do with being stable or not.

In the general teachings of one taste, you use any suffering you encounter to fuel compassion and bodhichitta. When you are capable of practicing like that, you will be happy to suffer. The result will be that your compassion and bodhichitta will increase.

On the other hand, in regard to rigpa, one taste refers to being able to recognize rigpa even while suffering. Pain doesn't exist separately from mind itself. There is no separate identity that really hurts; it is all simply one expanse of rigpa. However, recognizing rigpa, when you are in great pain, is not so easy.

Generally speaking, emotions are dealt with either as something to be rejected, transformed, or utilized as the path. Whichever of these you practice depends on what you know how to do and are capable of doing—it is a completely individual matter as to which of the three methods is best. We can discover personally, which is best for us by seeing the method that actually works when we become involved with an emotion. But in all three cases the essential matter is to maintain awareness, because without being aware of your situation, you will miss the opportunity to apply any methods. That is the main point, whether one rejects emotion, can transform it or utilize it as path has to do with one's ability to maintain awareness.

The Supplication in Seven Chapters known as the *Leu Duenma* says:

> Do this to whatever occurs in your mind,
> Do not lead, do not follow,
> Leave whatever occurs without adjusting,
>     without modifying,
> And when the mental movement dissolves in
>     itself, it is freed as dharmakaya.

However, that may not be so easy for all practitioners, especially beginners, so as a general rule the most important point is being aware or mindful.

STUDENT: How do I use painful experiences in order to be able to cope with difficulties?

Rinpoche: There is a particular instruction called *utilizing suffering as the path*. There are many different sufferings and painful situations, but as long as you have not realized the natural state, there is the all-pervasive, ever-present suffering of being conditioned. The only way to ultimately deal with such suffering is to realize the nature of mind.

There is a quote that goes something like this, "Once you know the nature of the painful moment, then it is not that suffering is some entity that is separate from the mind in anyway whatsoever." If you know the nature of mind then, as it is said, "Suffering is an ocean of bliss." Otherwise, not only is suffering painful, there is the emotional reaction to it, which makes it even worse and you are tormented not only by the suffering, but also from being emotional about it. There then seems to be no escape.

If one doesn't know the nature of mind, the normal way to deal with suffering is to try to exchange oneself with others. Do sending and taking (*tonglen*), and training in compassion. If one is capable of recognizing mind essence then, "A difficult moment's solidity falls apart, so that whatever is encountered is dharmakaya." If everything is dharmakaya, then there is no real suffering to worry about. This is the main intent of the one taste teaching, one aspect of which is utilizing suffering or bringing suffering onto the path.

STUDENT: Sometimes recognition is very easy and at other times very difficult. There are times when it seems so easy to recognize and thoughts are just liberated and vanish, but at other times it's like I don't even remember to recognize. It's almost like going blind. What is the best way to progress in such a situation?

Rinpoche: If this happens in the same session, it is because when you sit down you are fresh, strong in the recognition of rigpa, so that it seems very easy to identify thoughts; then as time passes it gets more difficult because you get tired and duller. If it is easy in the morning session and difficult in the afternoon, it is because you are getting drowsy. Whatever the case, please remember that rigpa itself doesn't improve or worsen, rigpa isn't sometimes strong and sometimes weak. Rigpa is the liberated state itself, it does not fluctuate. Any apparent fluctuation is most likely due to your physical constitution or state of health. In one of Milarepa's songs he says, "Rechungpa, my son, your view is like a vulture—sometimes you soar high, sometimes you swoop low."

# PART TWO: BONDAGE

# 8

# CHINESE INFILTRATION

When I was about twenty-three years old, I was in retreat and had several tutors. My senior tutor was a student of Jamyang Drakpa.[11] My junior tutor taught the yogic exercises in the retreat centers. He was in a room next to mine and on the other side was my brother, who was doing the 100,000 prostrations for his preliminary practices.

As I was in retreat, whenever any member of the royal family was sick I could not leave to perform the necessary rituals. Since my senior tutor was an important lama, he would go to the royal palace in my place. One day as he was leaving to perform a purifying ritual, he gave me a book and said, "When you finish your session read some of this, I would like to hear what you think of it."

Curious, when I finished my session I decided to spend my free time reading it. The text was about a particular form of Guru Rinpoche or Padmasambhava and bore the title *Drollo Namtar, The Life and Liberation of Guru Dorje Drollo*. But what was special about this text was that near the end it contained some predictions about the future told by Padmasambhava many centuries ago. Of course I had read biographies of Padmasambhava before and almost every one of them contained numerous details about how the Dharma would eventually degenerate, how people would be killed and Dharma centers would be destroyed, etc. These being Padmasambhava's predictions I never doubted that one day they would occur, however I had never thought that such a time had actually arrived. There was no way this could happen to us now: everything was fine, the Dharma was strong, there was no reason to think otherwise. Nonetheless while reading this *Drollo Namtar* I had the impression that Padmasambhava was not talking about events in the future, but rather those that were already taking place. Some of the indications were so clear that I got quite disturbed and began to feel that things were a lot worse than they seemed.

Upon his return my tutor asked me what I thought of the book. "I have the feeling that what is said here is not actually something that will happen in the future, but rather that it is happening now," I replied. Until then I had always thought that there was plenty of time before Buddhism would decline in Tibet, but that is nothing more than the usual tendency to cling to permanence and believe that everything will stay the same.

Soon after that I received some bad news from the Eastern region of Derge. The local chieftans and high lamas had been arrested, monks were being killed and imprisoned, and others were beaten up or humiliated in public. When word of this violence reached Nangchen, people got to wondering, "If that is happening just over in Derge, what is going to happen to us? We aren't that far away. What is going to happen here?" There was a lot of anxiety and uncertainty.

Up in the highlands along the Northern border was a Drukpa Kagyü Monastery in which there lived a lama who was said to have died and returned from the dead. After this happened, he became known for his clairvoyant powers. So several monks were sent to ask him what he saw about the future. He told them that within three years there wouldn't be a single person living in their monastery, and it would be completely destroyed. Some people believed him and some didn't, but everyone wondered what they should do.

I was twenty-five years old [around 1955] and pretty sure that anybody who stayed would not be able to fight off the invaders, but would end up being arrested, abused, and likely killed. We were in a serious dilemma as there was no hope of winning and no hope of staying, so what were we to do? Where would we be safe? In the *Drollo* text Padmasambhava said that the whole country would turn into a battlefield, people would be killed right and left, and the Dharma would be destroyed. When this happened he said the place to go was a secret place called Pemakö, Lotus-Arrayed Sacred Land. As India sounded too far away, I suggested people seek safety in Kongpo or Pemakö. But wherever they decided to go I told them that they should do their best to get away as soon as possible.

The Communists changed their tactics as they approached Nangchen. They offered the government officials and ministers high positions, and gave free food, clothing and medicine to the poor; therefore nobody felt threatened and everyone thought the Communists were treating us quite well. Peasants began to sing and dance joyfully in praise of the Chinese, making up lyrics about how the Chinese were like our kind parents and their influence like a divine gift equal to the Three Jewels. They just couldn't imagine how anybody could be kinder, and felt that if this was how it was going to be under Communist rule then that was fine. They couldn't have been any happier.

Slowly over time some education centers appeared, it started from the bottom up. The Chinese cultivated those in poverty, hence those who didn't have anything became dependent upon the gifts they were receiving from the Chinese; due to this dependency, they came to side with the Chinese. They were given everything for free, then were led to believe that it was people like themselves who were the most important. Those who were formerly in power but didn't take care of the people were oppressors, while religious teachers were blood-sucking leeches.

And sure enough over the next year or two, more and more Tibetans began to consider the local governments, lamas, and religious figures to be the enemy. That attitude became increasingly prevalent as the lower classes considered the upper classes with growing negativity. Gradually, many poor Tibetans came to believe that anybody who was not for them was against them, and to blame for all their problems.

Spies were sent out. People had to report to the Communist bureau. You never knew who you were talking to or who you could talk to—members of one's own family and even monks could be under the influence of the Communists. Over time we felt the restrictions tighten more and more until life became very difficult.

People had a lot of discussions about whether to stay or flee. We asked for divinations from a realized lama. It was reported back that for the time being it would be better to stay and bear it. Because of this reply some people suspected he was a Communist sympathizer, but people stayed anyway and didn't feel any great urgency to escape. However, word spread as random executions occurred but Chinese soldiers had not come to my monastery yet.

# 9

# FLIGHT

I couldn't make up my mind about what to do. At that time, my teacher Chögon Rinpoche was at *Dechen Chökhor,* his monastery in Central Tibet. I decided it would best to do whatever he suggested, so I sent a monk to ask him. I had made up my mind that if he said I should stay then I would accept my karma, remain and bear whatever happened. If, on the other hand, he said to leave, then I would pack up and go. The monk returned with a message saying, "It won't be good if you stay. But don't come here, to Central Tibet, as it is the same as where you are. The Communists are treating us just as badly here as they are there in the eastern lowlands. Instead of coming here, you should head south toward Pemakö, since from there you could escape to India. But whatever you do, don't come to Central Tibet."

I decided to do as he said, and began the necessary preparations for the journey. However, as I was the teacher of the king of Nangchen, I felt that if I ran off, the Communists would likely punish the king's family in retribution. So I needed to consult with the king before I left. The king said, "It would be better if you stayed. In the end, they won't treat us that badly. The monks will be made to work more and we will have to pay more taxes, but it is not the same as in Derge." I asked him why he thought this. He explained, "Because in Derge, they opposed the Communists from the beginning, while in Nangchen, we put up no resistance. The situation isn't the same at all, and it would be better if you stayed." I put aside my plan to flee and stayed put.

At this point we felt pretty certain that our monastery was going to be destroyed. Of course we had accepted that everything is impermanent, but there were many precious objects such as musical instruments, shrine articles, statues, texts, etc., which we thought we should attempt to save. We decided to pack them up and hide them up in the mountains behind the monastery. There were very good places to stash things where they would be safe, and when the situation was favorable again we could retrieve them to continue the traditions. Unfortunately, one of the monks couldn't keep his mouth shut. Word went out to the king, who then demanded that we not hide anything, for if we did, the Communists would get suspicious and the situation would get even worse than it already was. Hence in the end, the Communists destroyed most of what we had.

Despite the king's assurances, the circumstances continued to deteriorate, and eventually my tutor and I decided that we couldn't stay any longer. We contrived the subterfuge that I would go up into retreat to get some teachings and practice at one of our three retreat places. Thus my tutor, my brother, a cook, and I prepared to go up to the highest of the retreat centers by the lake. From there, we intended to flee. We couldn't take many provisions with us, however; we took only what we would need for a retreat.

This time the cook couldn't keep quiet. He shared our plan with one of his friends, who subsequently told the brother of the manager of Tsoknyi Rinpoche's monastery, who in turn told Tsoknyi Rinpoche. Later that day, an emissary came to tell me that the Tsoknyi Rinpoche, who was in his late sixties at the time, was on his way to meet me with a white scarf. I wondered why he was coming to see me. When he arrived he explained, "Considering the present situation I don't blame you for wanting to run away. But if you leave, I don't want to stay behind, you have to take me with you when you go."

"It will take a long time to make such preparations," I replied, "and I don't think we have that much time to get out of here."

"All we need is some food, clothes and a few provisions," Tsoknyi Rinpoche's manager interjected. "It won't take much time at all."

As we prepared, they kept adding more possessions, horses, yaks, and all kinds of other things they thought were important, so that before long an entire month had passed. Finally, the king caught wind of our plan and demanded, "No, you can't go! You have to stay, because if you leave then the Communists will surely destroy everything. If you stay here you will only be put to work and they won't really punish anyone. If you leave they will punish people and make our situation even worse. Running away is going to be worse than if you stay, so do not leave."

Time passed and, to allay the king's fears that the monasteries would collapse without their head lamas, the monks decided that they themselves would remain at the monastery and give the impression that their lamas were still there. With this assurance, the previous Tsoknyi Rinpoche and I finally got the king's permission to leave. So we left all our valuable possessions behind and departed the monastery with only one thought in mind: to save our lives.

Before leaving I also went to see my old khenpo. He was very sick and couldn't get up, but he told me, "I haven't been able to sleep much because I have been so worried that you would fall into the hands of the Communists. Now I am relieved to know that you are leaving. Once the winter starts however, though you may be able to escape the bullets of the Chinese, you will likely freeze to death, so please hurry and go as soon as possible!"

At last about a dozen lamas and monks were ready to leave, and the king offered us a *terma* statue of Guru Drakpo. The queen suggested that we use the pretext of visiting a sponsor's home, and from there, make our escape. That is what we did. After a couple of days of slow progress, we heard an unusual sound in the sky like continuous unbroken thunder. We looked up and saw a strange sight—an airplane. None of us had ever seen one before, and we didn't know what they could do. Some of us were quite scared, thinking that if there were airplanes, the army must be nearby as well. As the Communists were everywhere, even controlling the sky, it seemed that there was nowhere left to hide.

The Chinese now came in large groups called "armies," so "army" came to represent something dangerous. As we progressed we were able to avoid the Communist army, but we did run into the Khampa resistance army who were known as the *Chushi Gangdruk* (Four Rivers, Six Mountain Ranges), another synonym for Kham. We wanted to leave and avoid all conflict, as the guerillas were engaged in battle with the Communists and there was a rumor that young men who met the Chushi Gangdruk would be recruited into the resistance and we had no desire to become fighters.

However at a river crossing we saw the Chushi Gangdruk on the other side. We were totally exposed and there was nowhere to hide or flee, so we sent several monks across to talk with the general. The army had defeated the Communists in the Gonchok district and were on their way elsewhere. They asked who we were and where we were headed. The monks explained that we were fleeing from Nangchen because the Communists had shot so many people. The general saw that we were genuinely afraid and replied, "You don't have to worry about us. Go in peace and may you find safety."

The manager of Tsoknyi's monastery offered the general some brocade and money. The soldiers also wanted protection cords, amulets, and blessing for their weapons, which I gave them. The general asked if we had any weapons; since we did not, after a long discussion he offered us ten rifles in case we needed to defend ourselves. Since we were all monks and no one knew how to handle a firearm, we kindly turned down his offer. Upon hearing this, the general then presented us with five of his men to escort us safely on our journey. However, it turned out that none of these men knew how to shoot, either.

It took the Communists three years to completely take over. Speaking frankly, when people hear what occurred in Tibet between 1958 and the years to come, they have a hard time believing it. It is unbelievable, and the only reason I accept it as true is that I personally witnessed it with my own eyes. People who only hear about it second-hand find it hard to consider that what they are told is credible and actually took place.

# 10

# CAPTURE

Our journey continued through high mountain passes. We hid whenever necessary. We camped at various places along the way, occasionally doing various practices including a Milarepa puja. At that time we met up with the Queen Mother of Nangchen who had escaped, as had other lamas including Lama Chödak from Gebchak Gonpa, so we traveled together. Our plan was to cross into Kongpo to the south, because the Chinese army was already in Lhasa in Central Tibet. Along the way news reached us that the Tibetan army had clashed in a major battle with the Chinese. Apparently there were so many casualties on both sides that the blood flowed like a small creek.

One day we met two nomads, who, though initially afraid, eventually talked with us. They said that another lama from Kham, Khamtrul Rinpoche, had also passed this way

and that they had helped him get to Lhasa. Most of Khamtrul Rinpoche's party had been able to cut through the valley, but Khamtrul Rinpoche himself wasn't so fortunate and
the nomads had helped him take the high mountain route.
Once they were safely through, Khamtrul Rinpoche had told
the nomad, "If a lama from Nangchen should one day arrive
here, please help him just as you have helped me." When this
nomad discovered where I was from, he was quite happy
to help, explaining that it would be much safer to avoid the
valley and instead go through the mountains like Khamtrul
Rinpoche had. We discussed the best routes to take. He was
a great help to us.

Eventually we came to a fork in the road where there
was an ancient fortress; one road went south to Kongpo and
the other west to Lhasa. We then discovered that the Chinese
had not only taken Lhasa but the ancient fortress as well. As
Lhasa had not been an option for some time, we headed south
towards Kongpo.

On the way we met a government official from Nangchen
by the name of Urgyen Nyima. He told me that since he was
one of the only people who could speak Chinese, the Communists had made him the head of a district. Nevertheless, he too
decided to flee, so one day he had told the Chinese that he was
going to see what the situation was outside of Nangchen—
whether the CIA had infiltrated the surrounding area or
not—and preceded to escape. After settling his family in
India, afraid of what might befall the king of Nangchen, he
decided to return to try and save the king. On his way back
he ran into the Chushi Gangdruk and was told the bad news

that the king had already been captured. Knowing that being caught by the Communists was like being a fish caught in the jaws of a crocodile, Urgyen Nyima understood that there was nothing more he could do for the king and felt quite hopeless. He was happy to see me, and did all he could to help us, providing provisions, etc.

We went up to one of Jetsun Nyingpo's secret sacred sites where we decided to rest and do retreat. The Queen Mother of Nangchen, the prince, and Tsoknyi Rinpoche all came along. Urgyen Nyima had about one hundred soldiers camping close by, so he told us to stay peacefully where we were and not to worry.

While there one day I heard the OM MANI PADME HUM mantra being chanted and thought that even though it was at such a high altitude there must be other people about. "Is there anybody else around here?" I asked one of the monks. "No, that sound came from a bird!" replied the monk. Amazingly, it appeared that there were birds who could recite mantras, so it seemed that Jetsun Nyingpo has actually blessed this place.

During our stay there, other lamas passed through, including Zurmang Chögyam Trungpa Rinpoche. Sometimes, when we did feast offerings and gatherings, Trungpa Rinpoche would attend. He had a large following including many lamas and lots of yaks and horses. They traveled in a large caravan but every time that they crossed paths with the Communists, they had to get rid of more stuff. Sometimes they lost people; while crossing rivers some were carried away, and drowned. There was a lot of hardship and

Trungpa Rinpoche wisely let go of all his possessions, while other lamas clung to theirs and were not able to escape. So in the end it was just Trungpa Rinpoche and a few attendants, with no possessions, who safely reached India.

One time, when the Communists were chasing us, people were being shot and killed right and left, I did feel afraid. But when I actually thought about it, the fear disappeared. Fear would come suddenly when something happened. It was not like I was in fear constantly, they weren't out to get *me*; the soldiers were just following their orders.

Our journey was quite dangerous. The Chinese Red Army were always on our trail. Once I was with a group that came to a precipice, and I looked down at the scene below. People were fleeing from the Chinese soldiers who were hot on their heels, shooting at them. They reached the banks of a raging river and many held hands and jumped. Some women were so desperate that they took their children in their arms and leapt into the swirling torrent. Wherever I looked I saw death—people being swept away by the current or gunned down by the Chinese.

I was overcome with sorrow and tears flowed from my eyes. I felt sad for the Chinese soldiers. I felt extremely sorry for the people being shot down and the ones drowning in the river. That day, I shed many tears. I wasn't concerned for my own fate, because I had already taken my own death to heart. I did live beyond that moment, but for several days I was very saddened by the affairs of this world and didn't feel like eating at all.

Earlier on, when the Chinese were chasing us, people

were literally running for their lives. Whenever the soldiers caught a group, they would shoot everyone, including the women and children. People would see their loved ones being slaughtered right in front of their eyes. People suffered horribly and I felt extremely sorry for them. At other times the Tibetan army would kill a lot of Chinese soldiers and I found myself feeling sorry for the Chinese soldiers too, because they were not necessarily there out of their own wish. They were being forced to fight. They didn't even know whom they were killing; they were following orders and were afraid of getting killed themselves. Reflecting on all this, I couldn't help but recognize that the Chinese were victims as well. To be honest, I did have some bias; I felt more sorry for the Tibetans than for the Chinese. Of course I was sad when the Chinese soldiers got killed by the Tibetan Army, but more so when the Tibetans died.

I didn't get angry, because I didn't feel this was being done to me personally; it was more like the *concept* of lamas that motivated the soldiers to pursue me. There were so many others being harmed and I felt really sorry for the perpetrators. But it did not make me angry at all; I did not see a reason for anger. At those points that I feared for my life, I confronted my fear and thought, "What is the use of being afraid?" I knew death was inevitable, so why fear it now? I then remembered my guru, and my fear subsided.

What completely saddened and depressed me was that the Buddhadharma appeared to be reaching its end and was disappearing. Such a thought broke my heart, because the Buddhist teachings are the only thing that can really bring benefit and happiness. I knew that many of the monasteries were destroyed, and I thought, "All right, buildings crumble, that is no big deal. What to do?" But that great beings, meditators, hermits, and spiritual masters were being killed without having done any crime; I felt that was a great loss. It was like a strong wind snuffing out the flame of a butter lamp in which the butter hadn't yet burned down—the final age of the teaching hadn't come, but this was a major setback. I felt that that was a great loss, and it weighed heavily on my heart.

From Lhasa came the news of shrine objects and precious statues being desecrated and destroyed. Of course that saddened me, but I accepted it, knowing that all material objects have an end. However, there was an extremely blessed statue of thousand-armed Avalokiteshvara, which would instill spontaneous faith in anyone who saw it. It was said that when Songtsen Gampo had consecrated it, Avalokiteshvara's wisdom body had dissolved into it. So when I heard that it was destroyed, I felt this was a sign that Buddhism's demise was nigh and that now things would probably get really bad. I really felt sick in my heart and wept a lot.

During the two years that I was on the run, fleeing from one place after another, from time to time I would pass through an area where the early masters of the Kagyü lineage and other great masters of the past had stayed. High up in the mountains I would sometimes visit retreat hermitages that were blessed by great siddhas. Arriving at such places I felt, "Okay, I am being chased now, but so what? Let whatever happens, happen." It was so wonderful to be able to visit such places.

Ten of us had left Nangchen together, but as various monks caught up and joined our group, we eventually numbered about thirty. At one of our encampments, we had a discussion with the Chushi Gangdruk. There had been many Tibetan fortresses in the area, but one by one they had fallen to the Chinese Army. The Tibetan Army was still in control in Pemakö, which wasn't far away. However, we would have to get past one last Chinese-occupied fortress. The Chushi Gangdruk said they would try to capture the fortress so that we might safely reach Pemakö. We talked about this scenario at length, taking into account that many would lose their lives, while our escape would still not be assured. We would likely be hunted down even more relentlessly by the Chinese, not to mention that we would accrue the negative karma of being responsible for the deaths of many Chinese and Tibetan people. Though grateful for the offer, we decided not to proceed with such a plan.

The monks then decided that our best chance to escape would be if Tsoknyi Rinpoche, one attendant, my teacher, and I would go ahead alone. The rest of the monks could come later with the provisions, yaks, etc. They felt that their own karma would decide whether they themselves made it safely through. In response to this suggestion the manager of Tsoknyi Rinpoche's monastery said, "We came here with our possessions because we needed them. If we sacrifice these now, why didn't we just leave them in Nangchen? People shouldn't be separated from their possessions. They must go together."

Around this time, airplanes were occasionally seen dropping packages. The monks said they were from foreign countries, most probably America. Among the provisions and weapons, there were also gold coins, which made everyone very happy. They all thought everything was going to be fine. Now that foreign countries were on our side, the Tibetan army would be replenished, and the Communists would be defeated. At a river crossing, several other groups were also there waiting for a boat to carry them across. Since everyone was now feeling so confident, rather than splitting up into smaller groups, the ranks of our group swelled even further.

Everything seemed to be fine. All the Tibetans were joining together into an even larger group and people started to relax a bit. However, all the while, the Communists were gradually closing in on all sides. Occasionally, they would fire mortars at us. Our situation got progressively more difficult. We were forced to go higher and higher up into the mountains and forests. To avoid being spotted, we didn't pitch tents or light any fires.

One day as the Chinese approached, Tsoknyi Rinpoche and I, together with our attendants, became separated from the rest of the group, higher up on the mountain. People were scattered down below and throughout the forest. Occasional bursts of machine gun fire would shatter the silence. Every now and then a Tibetan would find us and tell us that whenever the Chinese Army came across any Tibetans it didn't matter if they were young or old, male or female, monks or laypeople, the Chinese would kill every last one of them indiscriminately, and move on searching for more. At one point, the corpse of someone I knew was brought to me and I did some prayers and blessings to help guide the dead man through the *bardo,* the intermediate state.

We stayed for two or three days at that remote spot. At night it would start to snow and all we could do is huddle there without a fire as the snow blanketed us. In the morning, Tsoknyi Rinpoche said, "Well, we are supposed to have tea in the morning, but we have no fire so what can we do?" A monk replied, "Can't we just swirl the tea leaves around in the cold water and then add *tsampa?* Wouldn't that be okay?" We gave it a try, pretending that it was very good to eat.

While we were sitting there, one of our attendants wandered off, leaving only three of us huddled in the cold. Suddenly we heard a sound, and when I turned my head to see what it was, I was looking right down the barrel of a rifle. The next thing I knew, five Chinese soldiers had surrounded us. The soldiers frisked us and searched through all our belongings. We had a rifle with us, but fortunately one of the attendants had hidden it in a bush so they did not find it. When they were done they began to march us down the hill.

My attendant and I were not that old at the time, but Tsoknyi Rinpoche was quite advanced in years and had difficulty walking, especially with the deep snow and steep, slippery paths. Each time he slipped or fell, the Chinese would hit him with the butts of their rifles or give him a hard shove. It was quite unbearable to watch and I wished that I could do something. Further down the mountain they put Tsoknyi Rinpoche on a horse, and to my great sorrow we were separated.

On a personal level, in a sense, all my worries were now gone. I felt quite relieved because there was nothing to run away from anymore. The refugees being chased, shot, killed, and drowned like the rush of one wave after another was much more disturbing.

# 11

# INTERROGATION

Eventually we arrived at an army camp. All the Tibetan prisoners were sitting in rows out in the open in the middle of the camp. Facing them was a line of armed guards with machine guns mounted on tripods. I thought, "Well, our time has come. There is no way out of this; we are going to be shot, just like everybody else." I had an amulet that would protect me from being harmed by bullets, so I was worried that the Chinese would find some other more painful way to kill me. Maybe it would be better to be shot. Though I felt the situation was hopeless, I prayed to my guru, Chögon Rinpoche, and that made me feel a little better.

Time passed and they hadn't shot us yet. One person from each row was taken inside a tent. We were all sure that they were going to be executed. But after a while they came back with food for the rest of us. That got me to thinking that if they were going to kill us, why would they bother to feed us. Maybe they weren't going to kill us after all.

At some point the Chinese soldiers told us that until that night, they were under orders to shoot on sight anyone caught fleeing. However, they had just received a new order only to shoot anybody who attempted to escape. At first we thought they were playing a cruel joke by giving us false hope and that they would shoot us anyway, but as time passed we started to believe that what they had said was true and we might yet survive. Then they threw us into a horse stall, which was used as a makeshift prison cell. They pushed people in until the stall was full. After that, they started throwing more people in, until everyone was squashed flat, one on top of another. Then they closed the door, and armed guards kept watch through the small windows. That is how we spent our first night in prison—crushed in a big heap.

By chance, I happened to be one of the people on the top of the pile. Light was coming through a crack in the door and suddenly the door opened and my father was thrown in with us. Later, my brother was thrown in as well. As we lay there, it got hotter and hotter, and it was difficult to breathe. It was unbearable. The people on the bottom were being crushed under the weight of all those piled on top of them. I was afraid they would suffocate.

Throughout the night, all one could hear was the moans and cries of people in pain. Everyone's crying out in agony and praying for deliverance sounded like the descriptions of hell. At some point, however, I did manage to fall asleep. I dreamed that the door opened and a tall woman with long, flowing hair entered wearing a blue dress. She came closer and closer, stepping on the people's heads and bodies, and came directly to me. She asked, "Don't you recognize me?"

I looked at her closely but didn't recognize her, so I asked, "Where do you come from?"

I am from *Kava*," she replied. I realized this must be the Dharma protector *Palden Lhamo*. She continued, "You have only one chance to escape. That is today. If you wait until tomorrow, you will not be able to get away." Then she left.

In the morning, the doors opened. They took us out in groups of ten, tied us together with our hands behind our backs, and marched us off. We came to a river, but there wasn't any proper boat to ferry us across—only some Tibetan canoes made from wood and hides. Warning us that if we tried to escape, we would be shot, the guards untied us, and loaded us in the canoes. When we reached the other riverbank, we were tied back up and forced to march on up another mountain.

One soldier guarded each group of ten of us as we moved through a thick forest. All of a sudden, our guard disappeared. I don't know why, but he simply wasn't there any longer. As the forest was quite big, we could definitely escape. My brother Chimey Palden and I discussed whether or not we should make a dash for it. Our elderly father was in one of the other groups and I was worried what would happen to him if we escaped. I told my brother, "He has no one to look after him, and we can't just abandon him. Also, if we run away and then get caught, they will surely execute us, and he wouldn't be able to bear that." Out of concern for our father, we decided not to attempt an escape, and instead caught up with the others.

In the evening, after walking at high altitude around one mountain peak to the next, we finally came to a plateau with some fields and a small village. There we sat in the field in small groups, surrounded by soldiers. Each prisoner was given only a handful of dry rice, which we even had to figure out how to cook ourselves.

The next morning we were woken up by a whistle and told; "Now it's time to get up and start walking!" Without being given any breakfast or even tea, we were forced to march onward.

For four days we proceeded like this, getting up at dawn and walking until dark without any breaks for meals until it got dark. From one morning to the next, we would get up at dawn and walk the whole day. It was very difficult and painful. Not only were our legs sore, but they started to become swollen as well. They got really bloated. Our feet were badly blistered and the sores oozed with blood. Everyone, even the strongest and fittest of us, suffered unbelievably.

Eventually we reached a well-fortified compound surrounded by barbed wire. We were all locked inside the enclosure, where we remained for three days. Everybody was in extreme pain. Our blistered feet were oozing with lymph and blood, and all our muscles were aching. We didn't get any warm tea to drink, only cold water. All we got to eat was two handfuls of rice daily—one in the morning and one in the evening—that we had to boil in a small tin.

Seeing everyone suffer, I couldn't help but feel that

whatever befalls you is a ripening of the specific karma that you created in the past. Of course I couldn't see what was happening in China, but I felt it was probably like this for all Tibetans. I felt very saddened for my countrymen who were also suffering in this way. But then I prayed to my guru, and did the sending and receiving practice known as tonglen, which eased the pain for a while. If the pain became overwhelming, again I made prayers and did tonglen. I was about thirty years old at the time, and to be honest, I suffered physically, but psychologically I was fine.

After three days of rest, I heard a strange noise that grew louder and louder. I saw these big objects move with something called a motor—I had never seen a truck before. They were really quite fascinating and scary. Five or six big trucks pulled up, and everybody was told to get in. Each truck was probably meant to hold forty or fifty people, but there were about six hundred prisoners and everybody had to squeeze into those six trucks.

We spent three days traveling like this to a Gelugpa monastery being used as a makeshift prison at Nagchukpa, north of Lhasa. We had never been in a motorized vehicle before. We were completely crammed together in the back of these trucks that moved extremely fast over rough roads, driven without any concern for our welfare. As we were violently tossed about, I thought this must be what the bardo is like, when the spirit leaves the body and moves through the after-death states, blown about like a feather in a hurricane. We were totally helpless.

Personally, I had no possessions, other than what I was

wearing. Because lamas, and especially tulkus, were singled out, I had been advised to dress like a layman, so I was not wearing robes. When I had originally set out to escape, I had dressed lightly, but was told that I should also take a sheepskin coat, since it would get very cold up in the mountains. Fortunately, then, I was dressed quite warmly.

The Chinese were not yet aware that I was a lama—I had merely said that I was the son of so and so, from such and such a place, never mentioning that I was from a monastery—but at Nagchukpa they found out; I don't know how. One day they read out my name and that of another tulku from a monastery in Nangchen, and we were told to come forward. We stepped forward and were taken around the back of the monastery, down an alley, and through some doors into a very dark chamber. There were some tiny holes of light at the top, but not enough to illuminate the room, so we couldn't see anything. As our eyes adjusted to the dimness, we discovered that numerous other lamas were sitting against the walls. No one was allowed to talk. If anyone said anything, from out of the dark a Chinese soldier would yell and wave a rifle at the offending party. We all sat there, quiet in the dark.

Eventually a Chinese officer came, scanned the room, and returned with two assistants carrying chains and shackles. He walked around, directing his assistants to put light chains on everyone's hands and heavy shackles around everyone's ankles. I had heard that being put in chains could be quite painful, with the irons cutting to the bone. I wasn't exactly afraid, but I got a little distracted and chanted some lines to *Mahakala*, a powerful protector. When the soldiers approached, they skipped me and went to the next lama. Everybody was handcuffed and shackled, except for me. As I sat there they didn't even look at me. I felt it was a blessing of Mahakala.

A whistle sounded; we were told to stand up. Somebody came in and took all the handcuffs off, but not the leg irons. We were told to walk out—everybody had to lift up the chain between their legs and shuffle out the best they could. Out in the courtyard there was a piece of canvas and scoops of rice were plunked onto it. We were told to sit around in small circles and eat with our hands. We got a little scoop of vegetables and some other stuff thrown on top of the rice as well. That was our meal for the day. There was one tap from which we could drink some water. We would all be marched over to a place where we could relieve ourselves. When we returned to the dark room, the handcuffs were put back on. As I entered I thought, "Okay, I escaped the first time, but obviously they will now see that I am not in chains." Yet to my surprise, I simply walked by and they didn't say a word.

As the days and weeks passed, people started to get lice, but they couldn't scratch themselves due to their shackles. The lice were gnawing away at them and they were getting really itchy. Some found it really unbearable, and asked me, "Please, please come over and scratch me." When the soldier was not looking, I would sneak over and give them a scratch, then the next person wanted one, and the next one. I spent the entire day going from one to the other until I couldn't move my arms any longer and had to give up.

There were so many lice that you could see them crawling on the outside of our clothes as well. The Chinese soldiers eventually got fed up with the lice, so they came in with a spray and fumigated everyone. The poison didn't seem to affect the lice, who continued to eat us even after we were sprayed. Finally, the soldiers set up large cauldrons full of boiling water. Everybody had to throw their clothes in to try and kill the lice. This improved things for five or six days, when the lice would again increase in number and we would be back to endless itching.

One after the other our names got called out and we were taken outside. We were taken to an interrogation room where we were asked our name, where we were from, the names of our mother and father, and our occupation. Everything was written down by hand and it could take a long time. When my turn came I told the truth in a very straightforward manner, explaining who I was. I even explained that I had had the name of a lama given to me, and I had been fulfilling such a role.

After the interrogation, you were taken out to the "struggle session," which was a public, mock court where you had to admit your crimes. If you didn't, you were taken back and beaten in private in the interrogation room until you couldn't stand; then you were carried back out to confess in public. You were always given a "free" choice as to whether you wanted to admit to anything or not. During the two months that I was kept at Nagchukpa, there were many trials. Everyone of any importance was put through a public charade of accusations. You didn't have to know or have even met your accuser, usually you were simply accused of acts that you had never done and knew nothing about. How many times you had to go through this charade depended on your karma. Anybody with any standing in Tibetan society, such as ministers, government officials, lamas, merchants, and property owners were put to hard labor such as working the fields with their bare hands

Eventually the trials quieted down and everybody was put to work. We were given shovels and marched out, armed guards following, with the command, "You will dig this area and if you aren't finished by this evening you will be punished!" We would work as hard as possible and do our best. While working, we could only see each other from a distance. Even when we were together, we weren't allowed to speak to one another.

We now got two meals a day: a handful of rice and a small scoop of green mush that was supposed to be vegetables. Since we had been raised on tsampa (roasted barley flour) and had never eaten rice before, this meal didn't go down too well and we had difficulty digesting it. In fact, the food was so bad that everyone eventually got diarrhea.

During our two months at Nagchukpa, we were tormented by sickness, malnutrition and lice infestation, until we were shipped off in various directions. Everyone, whether of high or low standing, was severely mistreated, except for those who had collaborated with the Communists.

# 12

# SENTENCING

One day we were all lined up and told that we would be sent home. Some people believed this and were really happy, thinking now they would be going home. What the Communists really meant by "home" was that we would be transported to prison camps in our own regions.

We were herded together in groups of thirty-six and pushed into the rear of a truck. Our hands were tied tightly behind our backs and we were forced to kneel with our heads bowed. We were stuffed together and told not to lift our heads, and if we looked up we would be beaten. It was almost unbearable. After a while people would lean their heads on the back of the person in front of them, or on the shoulder of the person beside them. For several days we had to travel like this, sitting in the back of a truck from early morning until late in the evening.

Over time it became very painful to have my hands tied with my arms twisted awkwardly behind my back, however I felt somebody gnawing at my ropes and gradually my rope loosened up a bit. The man behind me kept gnawing at my rope with his teeth, until finally I got my hands out and slowly brought them around to my lap so that none of the guards would notice. After having them tied for so many days and nights this felt much better. I couldn't turn my head to see who had done such a kind act, but later I found out that the man who helped me was an acquaintance of mine.

As we had been tied together in groups of ten and thrown roughly into the truck, we would land in awkward positions and often someone else would be thrown on top of us. Due to this, the ropes would become tangled up and get tighter and more painful. However, since my rope had been loosened, I didn't suffer from this as badly as many of the others did, just from hunger and thirst. The roads were in horrible condition and very rough, so it took seven days and nights to get to our destination. When someone died, the corpse was simply dumped out on the side of the road.

During the occasional stop, we were given dry tsampa to eat without water. We were given water only once on the entire seven-day trip on the road. We became very dehydrated and our lips and mouths became parched. The tsampa flour was impossible to eat without some saliva to help swallow, so we really couldn't eat. Because we couldn't move around, and the trucks were not covered, when it rained, we would open our mouths and try to catch the drops as best we could, even licking them off the backs of the others. As the elevation rose it began to snow and we would try to catch snowflakes in our parched mouths. Compared to starving, being thirsty is much worse. After a while your stomach feels like it is on fire, so everyone suffered terribly. About halfway, during a stop at Golmud, we were allowed to drink some water.

Finally we arrived in Xining, the main city in Qinghai Provence and were taken off the trucks and given water for only the second time in seven days. We were put into temporary encampments. It was very hot and we were forced to sit outside in the sun and again were denied water. Later we were given tents that were set quite close together, it was very crowded. In each tent there were six people who shared a single bucket for a toilet. We had to work under these conditions for two months.

After a while we were put into small rooms, with sixteen others. You could lean on a wall or sit and lean against others, but there was nowhere to lie down, so it was very uncomfortable. There were no mattresses, bedding, or anything else, only a can into which you had to relieve yourself right in front of everybody. Whatever clothes you had on when you arrived were all you had to wear. As the weeks passed, some people couldn't take it anymore. Some committed suicide by tying one of their sleeves around their neck and hanging themselves, others by smashing their heads against the wall. Many people took their own lives out of despair and agony.

You had to get up very early and then stand in line before the door was opened, ready to be counted as you walked out.

The first thing that happened was that you had to join a calisthenics group and do exercises. These were special Chinese exercises that everybody had to do. Sometimes, even though we were on the brink of starvation, we were also forced to do a compulsory dance.

After the morning exercises we were sent back into our rooms, then two from each group were allowed to go out to fetch breakfast. We weren't given any utensils, only a single cup or bowl. Our food was actually worse than what animals are fed. For breakfast we got our cup three-quarters full of boiled barley husks. This gruel looked quite filling, but when you dipped your fingers into it and squeezed it, you discovered it was like a sponge and didn't really didn't have any substance at all. For dinner we were given a few boiled tree leaves or soybean pods in a thin watery broth; often you couldn't even eat the leaves, so we just drank the water in which they were boiled.

Before eating you didn't feel so bad, but about half an hour after eating those husks you would start to suffer incredible hunger pangs. The pain and hunger would become so intense that your stomach would burn like fire. After a while, the pain would ease and you would just have normal hunger pangs and feel sort of spaced out and very weak. This occurred after each meal, but it was especially bad after the evening meal of "tree leaf soup." We lived on this meager diet for two years. I am speaking here from personal experience. I suffered, as did the others.

While at this place, we were again subjected to struggle sessions. Unlike many other prisoners who underwent repeated sessions, I only got pulled out twice. When your name was called you had to line up, then a main officer would sit there and interrogate you. Another soldier was responsible for whipping you, while a third took notes.

From the interrogation room I was taken to the whipping post. Hundreds of people were forced to gather around and watch. An officer announced what crimes I was accused of and I was asked to confess my guilt and repent before everyone gathered there, "Were you in the Tibetan army? How many Chinese soldiers did you kill? Were you a government official in your province? How many citizens did you punish, imprison, or sentence to death? Were you a lama? How much money did you extort from innocent victims? Now admit everything you have done!"

"I have never been in the army nor have I ever been a government official, so I have neither killed anyone nor passed sentence on anyone. Yes, I am a lama," I admitted before the crowd, "but I have never forced anybody to give me anything. I did accept what was freely offered, so perhaps I am guilty of accepting gifts, but these were all given out of people's generosity and by their own free will." Surprised by the insistence of my innocence the officer told me that I was one of the most stubborn prisoners they had.

"Certainly you fought against the Chinese army?!" he insisted.

"No, I ran away from you and fled into the mountains out of fear," I confessed.

They began to debate whether I was telling the truth or not, until one man turned and asked the crowd, "Well, is he lying or telling the truth? Speak up!"

A man from my home place, stood up and shouted out, "I know him. He's telling the truth!" Upon which he was accused of being in collusion with me, so the soldiers grabbed him and dragged him away to be interrogated as well. But then various other people stood up, about a dozen in all, and said that I was speaking the truth. While they were beating this poor man a sudden hailstorm swept in. The officer said, "We cannot work under these conditions, we will have to stop here for today. We will resume tomorrow."

The next day when I was brought before the officer, I was told, "Now that you have had some time to think about it, if there is anything that you did not admit to yesterday, now is the time to confess."

"Yes, I thought about this," I replied, "but I couldn't come up with anything that I haven't already told you. I do not have anything else to admit to." "Obviously you are one of those people who will not admit your true faults unless you are beaten," said the officer. "You will have to be put through some more public flogging." Before they were able to take me out and whip me, the proceedings were interrupted by the arrival of an important army general, and I was taken back to my room.

After a while, the day came when I was to be sentenced. Depending on what you admitted and what your crimes were, you would get a certain number of years: some got two years, some ten, twenty, or more. Before me, a lama got sentenced to twenty years—just for being a lama in a monastery! After him, a young monk who had been sent off to a monastery by his parents and who was little more than a helper around the monastery also got sentenced to twenty years in prison. Considering these harsh sentences, I thought that for sure I would get sentenced to life in prison, but there was nothing I could do but accept whatever punishment they gave me.

When my turn came, they falsely accused me of being a general from the Tibetan army, proclaiming that I had fought in two battles against the Chinese and had admitted to killing twenty-five Chinese soldiers. Not only was this false, but compared to the others this was a far worse crime, so I was quite surprised when they only sentenced me to fifteen years in prison. However, I never imagined that I could survive fifteen years under these conditions and with this food. I thought that I would surely die in prison.

# 13

# PRISON CAMP

Having been sentenced, I was sent off to a large prison camp that held about 10,000 prisoners.[12] When I arrived, there were more than four hundred lamas imprisoned just in the section where I was. Most were from the eastern regions of Tibet, but there were also some lamas from Central Tibet. The majority were Nyingmapa incarnate lamas, but there were numerous khenpos, geshes, and lamas of all schools of Tibetan Buddhism, Kagyüpa, Sakyapa, and Gelugpa and a few district officials. There were also about twenty Muslim teachers and some *Bonpos* as well. The experience of being inside the concentration camp was a very personal matter. Some people felt it was extreme torture, some medium, and some didn't suffer at all. It was very individual, according to the karma of each.

The camp was divided into sections. I was in section A, which was further subdivided into forty parts. My father and brother were in the same camp, though in different sections. Sometimes we would see one another, but we weren't allowed to talk. Sadly, my father died there.

In prison everyone had to work, without exception. Those of us who had been lamas were forced to endure the sufferings we had supposedly imposed on others. For example, whenever we got up, walked, or sat down, we had to do so in a line. Nor were we allowed to assemble in groups of more than two or three. At night we were not allowed to visit one another or chat.

We had to work all the time carrying stones and carving out part of the mountain. When you looked from a distance it was like the whole mountain was in motion because of all the people slaving away. We carried the bricks and stone to build the prison. The path was quite steep and treacherous, and if you slipped and fell no one would help you back up. The size of your meals depended on how many bricks you had carried that day; for example, for every fifteen loads of bricks you had carried, you would get a handful of rice. If you could only carry ten loads, then you got less, and if you could only manage five loads, you would be eating about the same as Milarepa—a bit of hot water and leaves. Because we had been starving for so long, we were only skin and bones, and we had to carry the bricks on our bare backs. After a while our backs were rubbed raw and the wounds started to ooze and bleed until finally one's entire back was a raw open sore, and one couldn't carry any more bricks. It was so bad that I still have the scars on my back. Your hands would become blistered and your fingers would also become raw and sore.

We spent our days doing hard manual labor while being starved to death—one's life was worn away from both ends. One day, while carrying a load of bricks, one lama simply keeled over and died. Later, another lama suffered the same fate.

Every day there were corpses in the cells. Each morning we would go out and line up, and whoever was left behind was either dead or had to be carried out. The bodies were thrown into mass graves, where the corpses were stacked one on top of the other. Those who were too sick to get up were taken to the clinic where they usually died. Every morning word would spread, "Did you hear? Eighty people died last night!" or "Only thirty people died last night—isn't that good news?" The empty beds were then filled with new prisoners, so that there was always the same number of us cramped in the cell.

A certain number of buildings were for the Tibetans and another lot for Chinese prisoners. But it didn't matter if you were Chinese or Tibetan—we all got the same tasks and lack of food. After a full day's work, we were not allowed to go straight to bed. Instead, every night, we had to attend "re-education" classes that lasted until midnight. We were told how benevolent and wonderful the Communist party was; America and other countries were criticized. For example, "Even though you were supposed to have been killed, due to the kindness of Communism and the Red Army, you were spared and kept alive. The horrible imperialists in America would steal everyone's possessions and suck the blood of the poor." We were also taught how to accuse our fellow prisoners. For example, if somebody had sat down when he was supposed to be working, we were expected to criticize him, demanding, "Why are you doing that?" Or if people spoke to one another, "What were you talking about? What are you thinking?" It went on and on like that.

Buddhism was relentlessly disparaged. Sometimes during these re-education classes, a particular geshe claimed, "Buddha Shakyamuni had been a prince and he only created Buddhism in order to protect his own image and kingdom. In the teachings of the Buddha, the junior monks must venerate their seniors and even wash their feet—you can judge by this what kind of religion Buddhism is! Monks must study for fifteen or twenty years, then sit and meditate for many more—and what do they achieve? Nothing! Emptiness!" Hearing this the Chinese were very happy.

Being imprisoned you are not physically free; other people decide what you do, where you go, where you sit, and everything else. Also your voice is not free, you are not allowed to chant or recite mantras and you cannot say whatever you want. But your state of mind cannot be imprisoned by others, only by yourself. The Chinese had no idea what I was thinking or imagining, so I was free to remember the Three Jewels, and I thought of them as often as I wanted. I was also free to remember my own root guru and do any other practices that I could remember as much as I could. There was nothing the prison guards could do to control that.

But that does not mean that it was not hard. Many people died, and each morning the guards would dispose of the dead bodies. Sometimes I would lose heart, but then I found it helpful to remember that I wasn't the only one in prison, there were many others too. There was no use fixating on my own suffering, because everyone else was suffering too, we all shared a general karma together. To worry about myself was like taking on an extra burden that made the whole situation that much more difficult to bear, which was pointless. There were also some incredibly great masters in prison at the same time who were really helpful. They could occasionally give advice.

# 14

# MASTERS I MET

Beginning in 1958 and the years to follow, huge changes swept over the districts of Tibet, which forced everyone—from high to low, lamas, ministers, government officials and commoners—to adapt themselves. It was often extremely painful for people to face these changes. The biggest change was the suppression of religion; therefore, those who had been involved in religious practices and study were subjected to the most severe repression. The ones who were treated the worst were those with a religious-political status such as those with an imperial seal of the priesthood and dominion from the Chinese emperor; there were eight with that seal, and four with other seals, I was below all these. However the Chinese had no way to discern lamas with qualities of learning and realization, so these practitioners escaped detection. Even though the Chinese tried to figure out who they were, for the most part, they were unsuccessful.

In prison camp, there were many rules that had to be obeyed very conscientiously. If religious followers broke one of these rules, they were punished much more severely than others. They kept a close eye on our actions and would not allow us to meet or talk to one another or exchange any news. Normally I couldn't speak with anyone, but every now and then during a major gathering I would recognize someone in the crowd. When I was able to get teachings from anyone, it had to be shared in secret, sometimes even while visiting the toilet.

Just the same, thanks to a monk from my monastery, who had already been in this prison for several years and had a good knowledge of the situation, I gradually learned about the presence of other lamas. I started asking him who was there and over time he was able to introduce me to about a dozen lamas. He told me their names, what lineage they were from, and whether they were of good or bad character. "So-and-so is a really noble character. But that person is trouble, stay clear of him, don't even talk to him." Gradually, over those fifteen years in that prison, I got to meet some of these lamas and receive a few Dharma teachings along the way.

During the day, all the healthy people went off to work while those too weak or sick stayed behind. One of those left behind was the incarnation of Dodrupchen known as Tulku Riglo.[13] He himself acknowledged that he was the tulku of Do Khyentse,[14] and like Do Khyentse he had supernatural powers and was able to perform some miracles even in prison. His Dharma protector aspect was particularly strong and he was able to safeguard people in the prison.

One day he apparently told those who were left behind with him, "Keep an eye out today, for among the new batch of prisoners due to be delivered I have a feeling there will be someone very special." After a long journey our convoy arrived. And when one particular truck stopped Tulku Riglo pointed to it and said, "I think he will be in that truck."

Aware that this tulku had some clairvoyant powers, someone asked, "But how will we recognize which of the prisoners is the special one?"

"He will have a round mirror hanging from his belt," stated Tulku Riglo.

That was the day I arrived. With our hands tied together behind our backs, we were unloaded from the truck. When I got out I saw the monk from my monastery anxiously looking at each prisoner. When he saw me, he wept. Another prisoner suddenly came up to me and said how happy he was that I had come, for he felt sure someone important was going to arrive. He had been worried since he couldn't find anyone wearing a mirror, until he saw mine hanging from my belt.

I made connections with several other lamas as well. From some I received teachings; others would ask me to compose things like a short Padmasamhava practice based on *Guru Mahasukha,* since I had done that practice in the past. Somebody else said, "If I don't die first I want to do 100,000 chants of the supplication to Padmasambhava from the tertön Chokgyur Lingpa, called *The Spontaneous Fulfillment of Wishes.*" Accordingly, I wrote a short version of such a prayer.

Somebody else said, "I had a vision of Milarepa, I would like a sadhana for him." Consequently, I wrote a short Milarepa sadhana.

The first lama who gave me teachings, however, was Lama Rigzin from Golok. Lama Rigzin had spent twenty or thirty years in retreat in one of Padmasambhava's practice caves at Mount Pomra. I wanted to meet him and so I asked my monk friend if he could help arrange it. One day when we went off to work, I found myself in the same group as Lama Rigzin. I wanted to make him an offering, but the Chinese had confiscated all my coral, turquoise, agate, and dzi stones; the only thing I had left was a *raksha* rosary that had a few coral beads on it. I undid the rosary, took the coral beads off and gave him the rosary as an offering. Lama Rigzin mumbled, "Oh, it's you. I've been expecting you." Apparently Tulku Riglo's word about me had spread.

Lama Rigzin was very dignified in appearance; he had a long beard, and was handsome. Even though he was very old and frail and had problems with his legs, he was still quite awe-inspiring. He wasn't a recognized incarnate lama, but was a very advanced practitioner of the togden (highly realized yogi) type. He was a disciple of the first Dudjom Rinpoche, Dudjom Lingpa, and knew by heart the condensed version of the *Nangjang* instructions known as *Buddhahood Without Meditation*[15] for which I requested teachings. "Don't worry," Lama Rigzin told me, "We have plenty of time. There is no need to rush as we are going to be here for quite a while."

It was not possible to receive detailed instructions in an orderly fashion, so we did it on the sly, in bits and pieces, which I got over a long stretch of time. Eventually, I got all the teachings on the preliminary practices, rushen, Trekchö, and Tögal, as well as the *mingling of the threefold sky*. Lama Rigzin had memorized all these teachings; I, however, had to write them all down in tiny characters on little scraps of paper.

One day Lama Rigzin told me, "I had a dream about you. I dreamt that you had a rosary made of silver. At some point the rosary came apart and you threw it into the sky where it turned into a dragon. It flew and roared, and all kinds of wonderful things rained down. This made me very happy, so please tell me something about how your writings are going to come out—do you have anything special?"

"No, I don't," I replied.

"Don't hide anything from me, just tell me!" he commanded, but at that time I hadn't yet received any treasure teachings, and all I could do was assure him that I hadn't.

No longer having a rosary of my own, I made a small one that I could keep hidden. During a search the guards found it and took it away, so I made another. The searches were always a surprise; guards would just suddenly appear and start rifling through everything. If they found anything you weren't supposed to have such as rosaries, texts, or naything else, they would immediately punish you. Inevitably, they found that rosary too, so I made another, which of course they eventually found as well. Finally, I made a tiny little rosary by knotting a small piece of electrical wire, and whenever there was a search I would slip it in my mouth and hide it under my tongue. All the others I made were taken, but this one was never discovered. I used it until I was released from prison.

One day I went to give Tulku Riglo the offering of the three coral beads that I had saved and to request teachings. When I arrived at his quarters he was not there. He had gone off to the bathroom, upon seeing me when he returned, he said, "I am very happy to meet an old familiar friend, Last night I had a dream that I was going to meet *Nubchen Sangye Yeshe*[16], so you must be an incarnation of him—mustn't you?" In reply I had to admit that in one of the supplication prayers to my lineage of succession Nubchen Sangye Yeshe was indeed mentioned, to which Tulku Riglo exclaimed, "This makes me so happy." Over time I received some teachings from him, not very extensively, but again in bits and pieces.

He was quite tall and very handsome, bright, and charming. Everyone wanted to be close to him. However, he was crippled and dragged one leg even while on crutches, so he didn't have to go work like the rest of us. He was one of the most impressive characters I met in the camp. He aroused spontaneous devotion and trust in whomever he met. While in prison he even revealed several hidden mind treasures. One of the stranger miracles he performed happened when he blessed some rice and threw it onto someone's robe. A few minutes later the robe started to move and turned into a snake. He then said, "Okay, the protectors are now inside the prison so you can take your robe back."

He was a very skilled artist and at one point said, "I have a present for you," then he gave me a beautiful line drawing of Samantabhadra with consort. Then from memory he recited the Guru Yoga of Padmasambhava written by Mipham

Rinpoche called *Shower of Blessings*, based on the *Seven Line Supplication*. In return he asked me to make him a line drawing of Nubchen Sangye Yeshe. Of course, in prison I couldn't sit and paint at my leisure, but Tulku Riglo kept asking for the drawing. Finally I succeeded in making a drawing and he was very happy when I gave it to him. He went on to tell me that, "In fact, there is another emanation of Nubchen Sangye Yeshe in this camp—you should meet him."

"Who is it?" I asked.

He explained that it was someone named Gyalse Palo from Golok who was a reincarnation of Gyalse Tertön, a treasure revealer. If I were to tell you his story you would be really amazed, but this is not the place. Actually this tulku was Gyalse Tertön's own grandson. He was on the work team and had to carry bricks and do other difficult jobs every day. I was encouraged to meet him, and eventually I did. He was very kind to me and we became quite close. At one point he confided to me that he sometimes got premonitions about what was going to happen, based on symbolic writing. Once based on such a vision he said, "I see that you have some hidden treasure teachings—have you written them down yet?"

"I have no such thing," I explained.

"Well you are probably just hiding them from me," he replied, "but if it hasn't happened yet, it is bound to."

There was another tertön in the camp as well. He had an odd name, *Tsokter*. His mother's name was Tsolmo, so he was named Tsokter, literally meaning the tertön of Mrs. Tsolmo, which is the funny way they named people from where he came. He was an unusual character. Some people trusted he was a tertön and others didn't, I myself wasn't sure, but Lama Rigzin told me, "You should definitely connect with him. Some of his hidden treasures are for real, others I am not so sure about. But some are definitely for real, so you should go meet him."

After I connected with Tsokter, he told me that he had a hidden treasure of *Dorje Phurba* (*Vajrakilaya*), which he gave me. It was *a* body mandala, which meant that the entire mandala was inside one's own body. When visualizing the various deities, instead of them being in a palace outside of one's body, they were in specific places in the body such as the *chakras*.

Every so often he would ask, "Are you reciting the mantra?"

"Yes, Rinpoche, I am."

"Okay, that's good for you; it's also good for me."

It was a very short chant so I tried my best to practice it regularly.

One day he told me, "We must perform a ritual exorcism also." This is called a *dokpa*.

"But such rituals are very long and complicated, how are we going to do one here in prison?" I asked. "We are not even allowed to sit for one minute, how are we going to do an entire ritual?"

It turned out, however, that this ritual was one that he had written himself and it was only the length of one short page. Next, there was the question of how to make the torma, the ceremonial offering, under the prison conditions. Tsokter Rinpoche told me just to find a small pyramid-shaped stone and we would use that. As he was quite old, he could only work for a short period, so one day we arranged to do the recitation for that exorcism while working. Tsokter kept the torma under his pillow for several days and recited the necessary chants to charge it before throwing it at the enemy. "It should be thrown at the main enemy," he explained, "in order to repel the hostile force."

"But when will we throw it?" I asked.

"Oh, at night time. It would not be good to throw it out of the entrance to the toilet, where we usually meet," he replied. "As we will not be together, please keep in mind that I will throw the torma tonight during the re-education session. Please, focus your mind and silently chant at that time."

The next morning when I met him, Tsokter was quite happy. "The torma went well and was quite successful!" he exclaimed.

Sadly, one day I received word that Tsokter Rinpoche had passed away.

Another teacher I met in prison was Lama Tsongar who was around fifty years old at the time. He was a Gelugpa and a very good person. He told me, "One of the most important things is to not create negative karma by nurturing hatred in one's mind towards the Chinese soldiers. Wouldn't it be better if we could use this opportunity to train more in bodhichitta?"

"Do you know *The Way of the Bodhisattva* by heart?" I asked.

"No, not all of it, only the first four chapters," he replied. Slowly he taught them and I wrote down the root verses. In prison there was no pen or paper, so I used scraps of paper torn from the margins of the newspapers and I would make my own ink using soot from coals mixed with water. No one was allowed to wear traditional Tibetan dress, so I would hide these small texts in the hem of my Chinese-style jacket. While I was in the toilet I would carefully pull them out to study them until I was able to learn all four chapters by heart. We weren't allowed to sit down and have formal teachings. Lama Tsongar would teach me in a whisper while we were walking or carrying our loads. That is how I got teachings on bodhichitta.

There was also a Gelugpa geshe who is still alive; he is ninety years old now and recently [around 2001] gave the grand empowerment for *Kalachakra*. His innermost practice, however, was the Dzogchen terma of the first Khyentse known as *Chetsun Nyingtig*. Sometimes this geshe would teach me parts of it, including giving me a commentary on the *Final Words of Senge Wangchuk*, the song of realization that Senge Wangchuk sang while passing into nirvana.

There was also an unusual lama, the son of a siddha from Tarthang Gonpa who had been the guru of most of the lamas in Golok. The siddha had several sons, and this one was also a siddha who, like his father, could revive the dead and perform various other kinds of miracles. He was also known to be able to cure people on occasion. Yet, even though he had performed miracles in the past, he too now found himself in prison.

The first time I saw him, I was coming out of the toilet and he was walking past. Even though I was a fair distance away from him, and hadn't done anything, he glared at me with an angry, accusing stare. I had no idea why. I hadn't done anything wrong, and began to wonder, "Is he an army officer? Is he coming after me because I did something the wrong way in the toilet"?

I got quite the shock when he then grabbed me and shouted, "Don't you know who I am? I know who you are, why don't you recognize me?"

There was another similar exchange, after which I wondered. "Who was that guy? Does he work here? Is he a prisoner or one of the prison guards? Or perhaps he is just a madman..." But then I began to speculate whether he might be the siddha's son, which could explain his odd behavior. I described him to someone and discovered that indeed he was the siddha's son.

Once when I got sick he came to treat me. He whacked me on the chest, and slapped me hard on the back, laughed, and left. I didn't get any teachings from him, but there was some connection between us. One day he said to his companions, "I am leaving camp now." Then he disappeared for a few days. He knew what he was doing, actually. He acted crazy but he was quite clairvoyant.

One of the lamas that I had the strongest devotion to was the great Dzogchen master Khenpo Münsel. During our years together in the concentration camp, he gave me many teachings. He also recounted to me the following story from his early days, about the unusual way in which he first recognized mind nature.

When he was younger, Khenpo Münsel's root guru was Khenpo Ngakchung. He received many instructions on the

Great Perfection from Khenpo Ngakchung and he had a very good intellectual grasp of what rigpa, mind essence, meant. Whenever he practiced meditation, he simply maintained that intellectual version of it and believed that that was what one was supposed to sustain. Therefore whenever he expressed his understanding he was able to explain it so well that Khenpo Ngakchung would acknowledge that that was how it is. Then one day Khenpo Ngakchung told him, "Yes, what you are saying is right, but you need to realize it also. It is not enough to know it conceptually. What you need to do is supplicate your root guru full of devotion and by doing so you will be able to bring it forth in actuality. You will truly realize it instead of just intellectually knowing it."

About two years went by and Khenpo Münsel thought he was making some progress in his practice, however he still didn't really get that his understanding was only theoretical. Then one day, the lord of Dharma, Kathok Getse, of Kathok Monastery, where Khenpo Münsel was studying in the philosophical college (*shedra*), returned after a long absence. In fact, Khenpo Münsel had never met him before. All the monks and students were told to line up in their yellow robes making what is called "a golden garland of a welcoming party." Khenpo Münsel was given the parasol and was really looking forward to meeting this great master. As Kathok Getse's retinue approached, Khenpo Münsel saw him among the throng, quite advanced in years. Khenpo Münsel was so delighted and full of admiration that as he looked at him something dawned in his mind but he didn't really notice it. He was so thrilled and full of faith and devotion for Kathok Getse Rinpoche; he just stood there.

Suddenly he felt a tug on his robe and he looked down to see a young monk, tugging at him and asking, "Hey, why aren't you coming in? Why are you standing here?" Khenpo Münsel looked around and to his surprise everyone had already entered and were sitting inside the temple. He went inside, sat down, and took off his ceremonial hat. Again he looked at the master's face and thought, "Wait a minute! What I have been experiencing here is not something that one does as a meditation. It is something that has been described to me, which I thought I understood, but all of a sudden I am actually experiencing it. This is what I have been thinking I have understood all this time, but now it is for real!" That was the moment when he recognized mind essence in actuality. The lama's mind and his mingled inseparably. Compared to intellectual understanding, this is called realization.

Later, he told Khenpo Ngakchung what had happened. "Your karmically destined guru is Kathok Getse," Khenpo Ngakchung told him. "He is the one with whom you have had a strong link for many lifetimes. Therefore the devotion and thrill of that admiration you felt upon seeing him was enough to make you shift from conceptual understanding into real experience. It is realization that is unchanging like space."

In this way Khenpo Münsel taught me an important lesson about the difference between intellectual understanding and true realization. Intellectual understanding is what you gain when the master describes mind essence and he clarifies it for you. He provides a clear description of how it is and you feel that you have a pretty good idea what it is. Then in your own experience you try out the method that the master has described, and you discover something. You feel "Hey, this is it!" That is called "recognizing mind essence." It is no longer an idea but an actuality. Once you grow so used to this that there is no doubt whatsoever, then it is not just a glimpse of recognizing, but an on-going actuality called "realization."

# 15

# HIDDEN TREASURE

Finally, I did reveal a hidden treasure teaching. It happened thanks to the immeasurable kindness of Samten Gyatso, who many years before had given me the empowerments for the Guru Rinpoche practices from the *Tukdrub Barchey Kunsel*[17] cycle. The Tukdrub Barchey Kunsel cycle contains outer, inner, and secret practices, as well as the supplication to Guru Rinpoche known as *Buddha of the Three Times*. At the time he bestowed the empowerments, Samten Gyatso told me to mingle the chanting of this prayer with my breath. I promised him that I would practice this extensively, to which Rinpoche added that it would be very beneficial for me if I did this practice in retreat.

This inspired me to quickly begin retreat. However, I discovered that I didn't have a copy of the practice texts. When I heard that Samten Gyatso had returned to his hermitage I sent a monk to fetch the texts for me, and when he brought them back I copied them and returned the originals to Samten Gyatso. Yet, when I was just about to begin retreat, an important Sakyapa lama came to Nangchen, so I did not get the chance to do retreat then.

Later I again tried to do a retreat on this practice but I had lost all the texts I had so carefully copied. I remembered that I had put them in the library, but I could not find them, so instead I just chanted the *Buddha of the Three Times* as much and as often as I could. It was during this time that the Chinese invaded Eastern Tibet. Throughout all of the tumultuous events that then ensued—first living on the run, then being captured by the Chinese army, taken to Nagchukpa, and finally transported to Xining and put in prison—I continually chanted the *Buddha of the Three Times* prayer.

Now in the prison in Xining, many people were dying daily. In the end, one epidemic hit in which I also got sick with fever and diarrhea and had to be hospitalized. In the hospital was a lama from Golok who told me, "I am going to die, but some day you will get out of this prison and after that you should go to Pemakö." A short time later he passed away.

Each morning people would come to remove the dead bodies, clean, and bring in other sick people; and so another lama from Golok named Lochi, with whom I was close, was brought to stay in my room. "We will both die, that's for sure," Lochi said. "I will probably die first, but if I live or die it makes no difference, I am not afraid." I told him that I felt the same. He then requested me to do the transference of consciousness for him if his time did come.

My fever worsened and I felt that death was very close. My temperature continued to rise and finally I passed out. While unconscious, I had a dream, which indicated that after four days I would know if I would live or die. I was pretty sure I was going to die.

The next morning I awoke and looked out of the small window in my hospital room and saw the crystal clear blue sky outside. I then had a vision, free of any grasping, of a distinct form of Padmasambhava known as *Guru Dewachenpo*; he was in fully ordained monk attire and was wearing a pandita hat. I didn't feel sick any longer, but I was certain that I was dying and wished to mingle my mind with the mind of Padmasambhava and eject my consciousness in the practice of *phowa*. I felt Padmasambhava sometimes to be close and sometimes far away until he finally dissolved into me. I then received the outer practice of Guru Dewachenpo, which I did not write down at the time, but since I knew it by heart from then on I would recite it daily.

All of a sudden I had met Padmasambhava, and by the second day of this four-day period, I was feeling quite comfortable and my sickness subsided. From then on my health improved very quickly. I remembered what Samten Gyatso had told me and I chanted *Buddha of the Three Times* all the time, to dispel obstacles.

When I was released from the hospital, Lama Rigzin immediately asked me, "Do you practice any heart practice of Guru Rinpoche?"

"Yes. I practice *Konchok Chidu*," I replied.

"Have you yourself written any other Guru Rinpoche

heart practice? If so does it have a seven-branch practice?"

I hadn't told anyone about my vision in the hospital, but somehow Lama Rigzin seemed to know all about it. Lama Rigzin had clear experiences and was highly realized; yet I was still very surprised by his clairvoyance, so I told him that I had received an outer practice of Guru Dewachenpo as a mind treasure. He nodded approvingly and said, "That's it! I dreamed you had received this."

He kept encouraging, almost demanding, that I not only maintain the outer heart practice of Guru Dewachenpo, but write the inner and secret practices as well. He even went so far as to tell my brother, "Because of the karmic link between you and Adeu Rinpoche, you have been born into the same family. Now that you are here together you must keep reminding him that he must compose the inner practices of Guru Dewachenpo."

In my past life, I had had another short Guru Dewachenpo treasure called *Dechen Sinnong*. When I was younger, I knew it by heart and this was very definitely the secret deity. Then one night my brother had a dream about the secret practice connected to this treasure. He told me that according to his dream, if I did not write this secret practice down myself, then he and I should write it together. I wrote what had been in the books I possessed when I was young—it was the same yidam as in my past life's treasure. I also needed to compose a petition to the protector for this cycle, Gonpo Legden. However, my brother was set free from prison and there was no one left to push me to write. I knew I should write this, but without being induced, I did not do it for a long time.

In the end I was able to compile the outer, inner and secret cycles of this treasure. This was initially due to Samten Gyatso, who told me I needed to recite the *Buddha of the Three Times* prayer, and later by the insistence of Lama Rigzin, whose clairvoyance did not allow me to let the teaching slip away. Lama Rigzin had requested me to practice this heart practice of Guru Rinpoche for a time immediately after it was revealed and also in retreat. He said it would be very beneficial for blessings and realization, so I have practiced it ever since. In fact, now in my monastery they do all these practices and there is also a sadhana retreat place dedicated to this particular practice as well.

# 16

# IMPRESSIVE DEATHS

An important part of my experience in prison was meeting a lot of powerful lamas who had control over their lifespan and their death. Some of these masters died in very unique ways, some sat in samadhi, a meditative state, for a long time. For quite a few, after they passed away, a beam of light extended above them directly into the sky—I saw this several times with my own eyes. Of course I always had confidence in practice, but the way these masters passed away brought me even more confidence in the trainings and the power of realization.

When the concentration camps were first formed, in 1958, the conditions were extremely brutal and many lamas decided to consciously pass away through the practice of phowa, the ejection of consciousness. Within my own section of the camp I personally saw five or six people who chose to end their lives using this method.

I also heard numerous stories from others who saw notable deaths. There is one extraordinary story that happened before all the lamas were put in prison. After the Communists took over a certain area, the lamas were asked repeatedly to come to special meetings. Ultimately, there was a major meeting where they all had to come. Among them was a special lama named Tsewang Rigzin who had been the head of the philosophical college in a monastery in Amdo. When he retired from teaching he went to stay in a remote hermitage in the very eastern part of Kham.

When the Communists forced him down from his retreat to go to the meeting, he was old and crippled. The soldiers tied him onto a horse by putting a rope under the horse's belly and tying the old lama's legs together to keep him upright. He didn't really have a choice but to sit there for the long ride to the meeting. Along the way, after crossing over a mountain range, the soldiers set up camp on the pass. It was getting dark and they left him tied on the horse while they took a break, relaxed, and had a smoke.

When they prepared to depart they discovered that all of Tsewang Rigzin's clothes were hanging on the saddle and the rope was lying under the horse's belly still tied to the old man's boots. The man himself however was nowhere to be found. They got worried and afraid, so they took their torches and searched everywhere, even up in the sky, but they couldn't find him. He had vanished into thin air, and since he was crippled the soldiers were sure he couldn't have run away. When they arrived at the meeting, they decided it was better to cover up what really happened and said that he had caused a lot of trouble and they had to shoot him.

There was another lama known as Kargo Tulku who was named after the place he was from, Kargo. He was a Drigung Kagyü lama and practiced in the lineage of Ratna Lingpa. He was tough-minded, stubborn, rude and fierce. He was definitely not a peaceful guy, but he had many disciples staying up in the mountains around him. After the Communists came he put up a fight. When he ran away from the soldiers, other people trying to escape joined him and they formed a resistance group. They became quite renowned for fighting the Red Army. So, in addition to being a lama, he became a military leader. He managed to defeat the Communists in battle on several occasions but eventually he was surrounded and taken prisoner.

They chained his hands behind his back and tied him onto a horse. Behind him were two soldiers with rifles pointing at him continuously while they headed towards the prison camp. When they arrived at the camp, the soldiers were shocked to discover that he was dead. His guards hadn't even noticed; he had probably done phowa. Even though he had passed away, his corpse was still sitting on the horse riding along fooling everybody. Upon discovering that he was already dead, the soldiers shot the corpse to give the impression they had actually killed him.

One amazing death that I personally witnessed was of an incarnate lama from Zurmang Monastery known as Rechungpa Tulku; he was the seventh incarnation in that line. I met him during the brutal trip when we were transported from Nagchukpa to Xining, which as I related earlier, took seven days. You will remember that our hands were tied and we were bound together in the back of the trucks, and we were not given anything to drink. On the bumpy road and burning sun, everyone was dizzy, trembling, and close to death.

Rechungpa Tulku was suffering miserably and in extremely bad shape. His hands were trembling and his head was shaking. He respected me very much. Seeing the state he was in, I felt unbearable compassion, and thought I might be able to assist him to do phowa, transferring his consciousness. I went close to him and said, "Now your body is too weak, there is no point in suffering like this. Wouldn't it be better if you just left your body?" "I don't think I can die for a few more days," Rechungpa weakly replied.

"Why?" I asked.

"After a few days it will be the twenty-fifth, which is a special day of Rechungpa," he responded.

It was true; the twenty-fifth day of that month was the anniversary of Rechungpa's *parinirvana*, passing into nirvana. It appeared that he wanted to die on the same day, so we continued on our journey.

A few days later, on the twenty-fifth day, in the sky above our convoy many circular rainbows suddenly appeared. Seeing them, I thought Rechungpa Tulku might be dying. A few minutes later the trucks suddenly stopped and we discovered that Rechungpa Tulku had already died. Normally the Chinese didn't even bother stopping, they merely tossed the corpses from the moving truck onto the road or into a river and continued on; strangely, however, they didn't throw his body out. They stopped and let a Tibetan carry the corpse a little distance from the trucks. Two armed guards accompanied him up a slope and after they reached a certain height, they yelled, "Stop! Stop!" But out of respect to Rechungpa, this Tibetan guy wanted to leave the corpse on the top of the hill, so he ignored the guards. The Chinese kept yelling, "Stop! Stop!" but he just carried on higher and higher. The guards got really aggressive and threatened to strike him with the butts of their guns. Finally, he stopped and left the corpse high up on the hill. When he got back to the truck, an officer said, "Here, you take this," and he gave him Rechungpa Tulku's coat. I was quite impressed, for normally, the Chinese were not so kind. Yet here they had not only let the corpse be disposed of with dignity, they also gave the man the tulku's coat. It was really quite remarkable.

What was most impressive was this tulku's realization, for how one dies is the ultimate test of this. There are so many stories of great practitioners displaying their realization by dying consciously.

Another event I personally witnessed was the death of Tulku Riglo. In the prison camp, people regularly died of starvation and various illnesses. However, when an epidemic struck the camp, people began dying in alarming numbers. During this time, Tulku Riglo fell ill, and since he was one of the greatest lamas in the camp, the Chinese told the doctors that they would have to look after him and make sure he didn't die. The Chinese doctor wanted to give him a blood transfusion, but Tulku Riglo didn't want any blood transfusion. He told the doctor, "I don't want it. I'll be fine without it." But because the doctors were on strict orders to keep him alive they gave him no choice. After the transfusion, he got worse and worse and his conditioned only declined. People said this was because the blood came from a Muslim butcher.[18] Gravely ill, Tulku Riglo finally said, "It is better if I die. I'll be fine after death and my death will be very useful. I may die but I have no regret, my death will be of great benefit."

What he said appeared to be true, for the day after he died, the epidemic started to reduce drastically; the number of people dying noticeably declined. His death was effective in that out of compassion, he had taken on all the suffering from the epidemic upon himself. His sacrifice was for the benefit of others.

While inside prison, Tulku Riglo had become close friends with another tertön called Lama Chinrab. They were both quite ill and one day they had made a pact to die together, but others convinced them to stay alive, so the two tertöns said, "Okay, if you are going to live I will too." When Lama Chinrab heard that Tulku Riglo had passed away, he exclaimed, "This can't be true. I don't believe it! We had promised we wouldn't leave without the other. He couldn't have left without me." But it was true, and the next day Lama Chinrab died too.

# 17

# RETREAT

A t the prison camp, there was a dispensary where you went to get medicine. The Chinese clerk spoke a little Tibetan, and though he liked me, he was very tough and unforgiving. As long as you were still able to stand up he would say, "Can, can! Go, go!" and send you off to work. If you didn't fall over, you had to go to work. One day I started to cough up a lot of blood, so much it filled several plates. I got dizzy and collapsed. I was put in the infirmary and was bedridden for a week. There I found out that the head physician had been the doctor of Chiang Kai-shek's son and the other details of his remarkable life.

During the Chinese civil war between the Nationalists, led by Chiang Kai-shek, and the Communists, led by Mao Zedong, our doctor was on the side of the Nationalists. At one point, he was stationed in a Nationalist camp that defeated a troop of Communists. Late one evening, he came upon two young, wounded Communist soldiers whom he treated and helped escape to safety. He kept silent about this encounter.

As the war raged on the Communists were eventually victorious; our doctor was captured, imprisoned, and sentenced to death. On the day of his execution, he knelt in a row of convicted prisoners awaiting death. Two soldiers went down the line, one reading the charges, the second shooting the condemned in the head. Onlookers watched the proceedings. When the two soldiers got to the doctor, a third soldier rushed in and stopped the killing. As the dazed doctor knelt there, the third soldier whispered something to the other two and pointed to the commander of the camp who had ordered them to move on to the next kneeling person and spare the doctor.

As they made eye contact, our doctor recognized the commander to be one of the young soldiers he had saved years earlier. The doctor's death sentence was commuted to life in prison, where he was allowed to resume his medical work, now under the commander. As the doctor was extremely knowledgeable and skilled, he quickly moved up the ranks and was at this time at our prison camp. He had written several volumes of medical treatises and was also highly respected, so whatever he said was taken as law in the prison hospital.

The doctor was himself a Buddhist, a practitioner who could recite the *Diamond Sutra* in Chinese. He was thus sympathetic to my plight, and announced that I had an incurable and highly contagious disease, and so could not work or be in contact with anyone else. He then arranged for me and six others to be quarantined together. One of us was supposed to fetch our meals, but because our breathing was said to be highly contagious, they were afraid that that we would contaminate others. So from then on they brought us our food. Actually we weren't very sick, the doctor had merely done all this to protect us. "Don't worry, you will be fine," he told us, "Just stay here until you are fully recovered and have all your strength back."

After being quarantined, the head doctor was our protector in more ways than one. He provided us with walking sticks and advised us, "When you go to the toilet, you can't simply stroll over there. You must look sick. Use a stick and act like it is a great effort to walk, practically dragging your body along."

That is how I found myself in isolation together with six excellent practitioners and important lamas, among whom was Khenpo Münsel. Except for trips to the toilet, I spent the next seven years in what amounted to a strict retreat with these great masters. We all stayed in a room together and did a session before breakfast, and then another immediately after we ate. We would take a break for lunch and in the afternoon we did our recitations or practiced in silence until dinnertime. In the evening, we would return to our practice until we went to bed. It really was continuous retreat.

During this time I got the complete transmission of the *Hearing Lineage* of the innermost essence of Dzogchen from Khenpo Münsel three times: the condensed, medium, and extensive versions. Khenpo Münsel said that the way he received these was by getting an instruction and then going off to practice it. Once he had gained some experience, he would go and relate it to his teacher, who would confirm or correct his practice. Then he would practice some more. This is how I, too, learned, starting from the very ground of the preliminary practices all the way up to the most detailed teachings including the eighth and ninth chapters of Longchenpa's *Treasury of Dharmadhatu* and its commentary, which Khenpo Münsel knew by heart. He also taught me other things such as the practice of Tögal based on the bardo aspiration from the *Nyingtig* tradition. I was very fortunate—it would have been hard to have such a long retreat as strict as that outside of such an extreme situation; it was all due to the kindness of the Chinese doctor.

At one point several of us got a strange sickness in which we felt pain in the head and shoulders. The doctor told us that our illness was not normal but a kind of defilement; therefore we recited a special vajra *dharani* mantra of *Vajravidarana* for purification. Even when recited very fast, the long version of this mantra takes more than three minutes to complete. We repeated it 100,000 times, and the short version many millions of times. The doctor gave us some sugar that we blessed during the recitation. We were not sure exactly when, but all of our symptoms disappeared and we all got healthy. After that none of us really got sick again in the following years. I kept some of that sugar and still have some [2002] that I use a little bit of during purification and cleansing rituals.

Another time, an epidemic spread in the camp and many people died. One governor from Golok, who was also a lama, said that a particular medical treasure from King Gesar was needed in order to remedy the situation. Years before the Chinese invasion, I had been told the story about how King Gesar had discovered this medicine treasure. The original text of this tale had been lost, but a lama remembered the story and I had written it down while he told it many years ago. I no longer had my copy, but while I was "quarantined" with the others, this governor asked if I could remember what the text contained. Unfortunately I had to admit that I couldn't remember, but as he kept insisting I did my best and began to write what little I could recall. I wrote on small strips of paper that I rolled up and hid in the bottom of a jar of brown sugar. Oddly, as I wrote, more and more of the story came back to me. I was amazed when I realized that I had about half of it written down again. I would write down a sentence, then the next one would come naturally almost automatically. It just kept going until I was able to complete the entire story, which made for quite a long book. Surprisingly, when I finished, the sickness started to disappear and the epidemic soon passed.

Once a month or so, guards braved coming into our room and searched everything, but they never looked in the jar where the text was hidden. That is how we still have this story entitled *Shangshang Mesel*.

One day Khenpo Münsel said, "This year is a special year, for it is the monkey year [1980], and the anniversary of Padmasambhava, the tenth day of the monkey month, is coming up. Before that we must accumulate recitations of the *Seven Line Supplication to Guru Rinpoche*." Everybody did 100,000.

Then he said we must do some *Buddha of the Three Times* supplications, and we all did 100,000 of those as well. "Before the tenth day of the monkey month," he then said, "We should accumulate a great number of feast offerings." Of course we didn't really have anything to give as offerings; however, we were paid one Yuan of Chinese money[19] per month for our labor, which we usually used to buy some sugar, fruit, or the like. We pooled our resources and managed to buy a few things. The doctor got us some tsampa that we molded into offering objects and put on a makeshift shrine we had hidden behind some cloth.

Whenever the doctor came in, he would cover his mouth and fumigate ahead of him. Therefore everyone was afraid to put even a foot into our room. But on the eighth day of the Tibetan calendar, the offerings began to smell strange, and on the ninth day an odor like medicinal herbs, sort of like the blessed medicine known as *mendrup*, had gotten quite strong. The doctor came and told us, "I can smell this from a long way outside the hospital and have been trying to find out where it was coming from, and now I discover it is coming from your room. Whatever do you have in here?" We explained that we didn't have anything special, just a few pieces of fruit and some barley flour.

The smell, however, got stronger and stronger, and on the morning of the tenth, when we uncovered the shrine, all the fruit, tsampa, and other things, which we had placed there had this smell—a very strong, sweet scent of mendrup. Even for a long time afterward, just a small piece of it would retain that scent. Personally, I thought this was pretty unusual.

After about seven years, the day arrived when the Chinese doctor came and said, "I have tried my best, but I cannot keep you here any longer, because they say all prisoners must be kept with the main group." So our "retreat" ended and we were taken out and put in a less strict section of the prison where you didn't need permission simply to pee.

When I think about my years in prison, they were painful but also fortunate. I connected with incredible lamas, received some teachings, and was able to practice the Dharma. I was finally released from prison altogether after staying in the less strict section for one year. Later, Khenpo Münsel was also set free. At last, not long after being released, I was permitted to go to Nangchen Gar; it had been twenty-four years since I had last seen my home.

# ACKNOWLEDGEMENTS

Many sincere words of appreciation go to everyone who helped with this book. Firstly to Tsoknyi Rinpoche for agreeing to let it be published and giving his foreword; to Erik Pema Kunsang for precise, clear translating; to Michael Tweed for transcribing some of the tapes, editing and rearranging the book to make it more cohesive and readable; to Laura Dainty for transcribing the rest of the tapes; to David Leskowitz for copy editing; to Joan Olson for book design and type setting; to Maryann Lipaj for her beautiful cover; and to Carol Schlenger, Gloria Jones and Zack Beer for proof reading.

Teachers and practitioners like Adeu Rinpoche are rare in this world, may his words meet with worthy students who may be immensely benefited.

# Notes

1. See Tulku Urgyen Rinpoche, *Blazing Splendor* (Hong Kong: Rangjung Yeshe Publications, 2005), p. 370–371.
2. Ibid., 379, footnote 72. Padmasambhava's prophecies tend to be very precise; it was even predicted in the terma itself that "within one to three years he should be given this terma."
3. Qinghai Provence, China.
4. Op cit., 129. Shakya Shri, the Lord of Siddhas. *Togden* means "to possess realization," p.129.
5. The fourth of the four mind changings is the sufferings of samsara.
6. Reproduced from *Quintessential Dzogchen* (Hong Kong: Rangjung Yeshe Publications, 2006), p. 208
7. The *Seven Notions* or *Seven Enquiries*, the root tantra of Bhairava.
8. Erik Pema Kunsang, trans. *The Light of Wisdom* (Hong Kong: Rangjung Yeshe Publications, 2004. *Skillful Grace The Essential Instruction in the Threefold Excellence* (Hong Kong: Rangjung Yeshe Publications, 2007).
9. The phrase "to offer one's realization" refers to the tradition of describing one's experience of the natural state (rigpa) to a meditation master so that he can validate it. Once it has gotten the stamp of approval, then comes the main practice of training in rigpa to attain stability.

10. The *Tigle Gyachen* is the guru sadhana of Longchen Rabjam.

11. See Tulku Urgyen Rinpoche, *Blazing Splendor* Master in the Hollow Tree. p. 215

12. Tulku Thondup, *Masters of Meditation and Miracles*, (Boston: Shambhala Publications, 1996), p. 310. "This camp was one of the most infamous, massive prison camps in the barren landscape of Qinghai. Most prisoners had to work at hard labor. Because of the prison system, the prisoners mostly had to live on thin gruel. It was a place for slow death by hunger and labor, not so much by the torture of beating."

13. Rigzin Tenpe Gyaltsen (1927–1961).

14. A great master who lived during the 19th century in eastern Tibet.

15. Lingpa, Dudjom. *Buddhahood Without Meditation: A Visionary Account known as Refining One's Perception (Nang-jang)*. Translated by Richard Barron (Chökyi Nyima) (Junction City: Padma Publishing, 2002).

16. One of the original twenty-five disciples of Padmasambhava in the 9th century in central Tibet.

17. A combined hidden treasure cycle of teachings from Chokgyur Dechen Lingpa and Jamyang Khyentse Wangpo revealed in the middle of the 19th century.

18. Tulku Thondup, *Masters of Meditation and Miracles*, p. 310.

19. There are 8 yuan to the U.S. dollar.